MACHINE LEARNING FOR BEGINNERS

A Comprehensive Guide

MAXWELL RIVERS

INTRODUCTION

In the rapidly evolving world of technology, the term "machine learning" has become increasingly prevalent. From self-driving cars to personalized recommendations on streaming platforms, machine learning is behind many of the innovations that shape our daily lives. It's the driving force behind the intelligent systems that make predictions, recognize patterns, and solve complex problems without explicit programming.

But what exactly is machine learning, and why should you, as a beginner, care about it?

Imagine having the ability to teach a computer to learn from data and make decisions based on that learning. Machine learning, at its core, is this art of teaching computers to learn and adapt, much like how humans learn from experience. It's the science of giving computers the ability to improve their performance on a task as they gain more experience with it.

Whether you're a student looking to start your career in artificial intelligence, a professional seeking to enhance your skills, or simply someone fascinated by the possibilities of technology, this book is designed to be your comprehensive guide.

Why Learn Machine Learning?

The reasons for learning machine learning are as diverse as the applications of the technology itself. Here are a few compelling motivations:

1. **Solve Real-World Problems**: Machine learning can be applied to a wide range of domains, from healthcare and finance to marketing and entertainment. By understanding machine learning, you gain the tools to address real-world challenges and create innovative solutions.

2. **Career Opportunities**: Machine learning is in high demand across industries. Learning this skill can open up exciting career opportunities, with companies actively seeking professionals who can harness the power of data and machine learning to drive business success.

3. **Empowerment**: As technology becomes increasingly integrated into our lives, understanding how machine learning works empowers you to make informed decisions about the products and services you use. It also enables you to engage in discussions about the ethical and societal implications of AI and machine learning.

4. **Personal Growth**: Learning machine learning is a journey of personal growth and intellectual exploration. It challenges your problem-solving abilities, encourages critical thinking, and fosters creativity in solving complex problems.

Prerequisites for this Book

You might be wondering if you need a background in mathematics or computer science to delve into machine learning. While some familiarity with these subjects can be helpful, this book is designed to cater to beginners with varying levels of prior knowledge. We'll start with the fundamentals and gradually build your understanding, ensuring that you can grasp the concepts even if you're new to the field.

Throughout this book, we'll use plain language and practical examples to explain complex concepts. You don't need an advanced degree or specialized expertise to follow along. All that's required is a curious mind and a willingness to learn.

CONTENTS

GETTING STARTED WITH MACHINE LEARNING

The Basics of Data

In machine learning, data is the foundation upon which all intelligent systems are built. It's crucial to grasp the fundamentals of data—what it is, where it comes from, and why it's so essential in the context of machine learning.

What is Data?

Data, in its most general form, refers to information. It can take various shapes and sizes, ranging from numbers and text to images, audio, and more. In the context of machine learning, data is the raw material that algorithms use to learn patterns, make predictions, or solve problems. This data can come from a multitude of sources, such as sensors, databases, user interactions, and the internet.

Consider, for instance, a recommendation system on your favorite streaming platform. It analyzes data about your viewing history, the content you've liked or disliked, and the behaviors of millions of other users to suggest movies or shows you might enjoy. In this case, data consists of everything from the titles of movies to the timestamps of your interactions.

Types of Data

Data can be categorized into various types, which dictate how it is collected, stored, and processed. Understanding these types is crucial for handling data effectively in machine learning:

1. **Numerical Data**: This type of data consists of numbers and is commonly used in quantitative analysis. Examples include stock prices, temperatures, and customer ages.
2. **Categorical Data**: Categorical data represents distinct categories or labels. It includes data like product categories, gender, or city names. Categorical data can be further divided into nominal (categories without any inherent order) and ordinal (categories with a specific order) data.
3. **Text Data**: Text data comprises written or spoken words and is prevalent in natural language processing tasks such as sentiment analysis, chatbots, and language translation.
4. **Image Data**: Images, as a form of data, consist of pixel values and are used in computer vision tasks like object detection, facial recognition, and image classification.
5. **Audio Data**: Audio data represents sound waves and is utilized in applications like speech recognition, music classification, and audio generation.

Why Data is Crucial in Machine Learning

Data is the fuel that powers machine learning algorithms. Without sufficient and relevant data, even the most advanced algorithms are powerless. Here's why data is so essential:

1. **Pattern Recognition**: Machine learning algorithms excel at recognizing patterns within data. They use these patterns to make predictions, classify objects, or detect anomalies.
2. **Generalization**: The ability of algorithms to generalize from data allows them to perform well on unseen examples. This is crucial for making models that work in the real world.
3. **Continuous Learning**: Machine learning models can adapt and improve their performance over time as they receive

more data. This ability to learn from experience is a hallmark of machine learning.

4. **Decision-Making**: In many applications, machine learning models are used to make data-driven decisions. The quality of these decisions depends on the quality of the data.

Types of Machine Learning

Machine learning is a vast and dynamic field that encompasses various approaches to solving problems and making predictions. Understanding the different types of machine learning is crucial as it provides insight into the techniques used to teach computers to learn from data.

1. Supervised Learning

Supervised learning is one of the most common types of machine learning. In this approach, the algorithm is trained on a labeled dataset, which means that the input data is paired with the correct output or target. The goal is for the algorithm to learn the mapping between inputs and outputs so that it can make predictions or classifications when presented with new, unlabeled data.

Common applications of supervised learning include:

- **Classification**: Assigning inputs to predefined categories. For example, classifying emails as spam or not spam.
- **Regression**: Predicting a continuous output. For instance, predicting house prices based on features like square footage and number of bedrooms.

2. Unsupervised Learning

Unsupervised learning deals with unlabeled data, where the algorithm is tasked with finding patterns, structures, or relationships within the data without explicit guidance. This type of learning is often used for data exploration and clustering, where the algorithm groups similar data points together based on their inherent similarities.

Common applications of unsupervised learning include:

- **Clustering**: Grouping similar data points together, such as clustering customers by purchasing behavior.
- **Dimensionality Reduction**: Reducing the complexity of data while preserving essential information, as in Principal Component Analysis (PCA).

3. Semi-Supervised Learning

Semi-supervised learning is a hybrid approach that combines elements of both supervised and unsupervised learning. It leverages a dataset that contains both labeled and unlabeled examples. The algorithm uses the labeled data for guidance and the unlabeled data for discovering patterns or refining its predictions.

Semi-supervised learning is particularly useful when obtaining labeled data is expensive or time-consuming, as it can make the most of available resources.

4. Reinforcement Learning

Reinforcement learning is a type of machine learning where an agent interacts with an environment and learns to make a sequence of decisions to maximize a reward. The agent takes actions and receives feedback in the form of rewards or penalties based on its actions. Over time, it learns to take actions that lead to higher rewards.

Applications of reinforcement learning include:

- **Game Playing**: Achieving superhuman performance in games like chess, Go, and video games.
- **Robotics**: Teaching robots to perform tasks by trial and error, such as autonomous navigation.

5. Self-Supervised Learning

Self-supervised learning is a relatively new approach where models are trained on data without external labels. Instead, the models generate their own labels from the data, creating a self-imposed supervision signal. This method has shown promise in various natural language processing and computer vision tasks.

6. Transfer Learning

Transfer learning involves training a model on one task and then applying the knowledge gained to a related but different task. This is particularly useful when you have limited data for the target task. Pretrained models, such as those used in deep learning, are often fine-tuned for specific tasks using transfer learning.

7. Online and Batch Learning

Machine learning systems can be categorized as online or batch learners:

- **Online Learning**: In online learning, the model is updated continuously as new data arrives. It adapts to changing conditions and can be well-suited for real-time applications like recommendation systems.
- **Batch Learning**: In batch learning, the model is trained on a fixed dataset and then applied to new data without further updates. This approach is common for tasks like batch processing of large datasets.

The Machine Learning Workflow

Machine learning is not just about training models; it's a structured process that involves several stages, from data preparation to model deployment. Understanding the machine learning workflow is essential for anyone looking to apply machine learning effectively.

1. Data Collection and Acquisition

The journey into machine learning often begins with data. Collecting and acquiring the right data is the foundational step. This involves determining what data is needed for the task at hand, sourcing the data from various sources, and ensuring that the data is clean, reliable, and representative of the problem you want to solve.

2. Data Preprocessing

Raw data is rarely in perfect form for machine learning. Data preprocessing is the process of cleaning, transforming, and organizing the data to make it suitable for training machine learning models. This stage involves tasks like handling missing values, encoding categorical variables, and scaling numerical features.

3. Data Splitting

Before training a machine learning model, it's common practice to split the dataset into at least two subsets: a training set and a testing set. The training set is used to train the model, while the testing set is reserved to evaluate the model's performance. In some cases, a validation set is used for hyperparameter tuning.

4. Model Selection and Training

Once the data is prepared, you select a machine learning algorithm or model that is appropriate for your task. The chosen model is trained on the training data, which involves finding the patterns and relationships within the data. The training process aims to minimize the model's error or loss function.

5. Model Evaluation

After training, the model's performance is assessed using the testing dataset. Various evaluation metrics are used depending on the type of machine learning problem. For classification tasks, metrics like accuracy, precision, recall, and F1-score are common. For regression, metrics like mean squared error (MSE) or root mean squared error (RMSE) are used.

6. Hyperparameter Tuning

Models often have hyperparameters that are not learned during training but must be set before training begins. Hyperparameter tuning involves optimizing these settings to improve the model's performance. Techniques like grid search, random search, and Bayesian optimization are commonly used for hyperparameter tuning.

7. Model Deployment

Once you have a well-trained and evaluated model, the next step is deploying it to a production environment where it can make predictions on new, unseen data. Deployment can vary from embedding the model in a mobile app to integrating it into a web service or a larger software system.

8. Monitoring and Maintenance

After deployment, it's crucial to monitor the model's performance in real-world scenarios. Models can drift over time, meaning they may become less accurate as data distributions change. Regular maintenance and retraining may be necessary to ensure the model continues to perform well.

9. Interpretability and Explainability

Understanding why a model makes a particular prediction is essential, especially in applications where decisions have real-world consequences. Interpretability and explainability techniques help provide insights into how the model arrived at its conclusions.

10. Scaling and Optimization

As your machine learning projects grow in complexity and scale, you may need to consider scaling your infrastructure to handle larger datasets and more significant workloads. This involves optimizing both the training and inference processes.

11. Ethical Considerations

Throughout the entire machine learning workflow, ethical considerations should be kept in mind. Bias in data, fairness, transparency, and accountability are vital aspects to consider when designing, training, and deploying machine learning models.

Tools and Software for Machine Learning

Machine learning is a multidisciplinary field that relies heavily on software and tools to develop, train, and deploy models effectively.

1. Programming Languages

Python: Python is the most popular programming language for machine learning. It offers a rich ecosystem of libraries and frameworks that simplify the implementation of machine learning algorithms. Some key libraries include NumPy (for numerical operations), pandas (for data manipulation), scikit-learn (for machine learning algorithms), TensorFlow, and PyTorch (for deep learning).

R: R is another programming language used for statistical analysis and machine learning. It's particularly strong in data visualization and statistical modeling. The "caret" package in R is known for its versatility in training and evaluating machine learning models.

2. Integrated Development Environments (IDEs)

Jupyter Notebook: Jupyter Notebook is a popular choice for developing and documenting machine learning projects. It provides an interactive environment where you can write code, visualize results, and add explanatory text all in one place. It's especially well-suited for exploratory data analysis.

PyCharm, Visual Studio Code, RStudio: These IDEs offer excellent support for Python and R programming, making them convenient choices for developing machine learning projects. They come with features like code debugging, version control integration, and extensions for machine learning libraries.

3. Data Visualization Tools

Matplotlib: Matplotlib is a powerful library for creating static, animated, and interactive visualizations in Python. It's commonly used for plotting data distributions, trends, and model performance metrics.

Seaborn: Seaborn is a Python data visualization library built on top of Matplotlib. It simplifies the creation of attractive statistical graphics and works well with pandas data structures.

Tableau, Power BI: These commercial tools are excellent choices for creating interactive data dashboards and visualizations. They are commonly used for exploring and presenting insights from data.

4. Machine Learning Frameworks

scikit-learn: Scikit-learn is a popular machine learning library for Python. It provides a wide range of algorithms for classification, regression, clustering, dimensionality reduction, and more. Scikit-learn is known for its simple and consistent API.

TensorFlow and PyTorch: These deep learning frameworks are widely used for building and training neural networks. They offer flexibility and scalability for deep learning tasks and have large and active communities.

5. Data Preparation and Cleaning Tools

OpenRefine: OpenRefine is an open-source tool for data cleaning and transformation. It helps users explore and clean messy data efficiently.

Trifacta, DataRobot: Commercial tools like Trifacta and DataRobot offer data wrangling and feature engineering capabilities to streamline the data preparation process.

6. Cloud Platforms

Amazon Web Services (AWS), Google Cloud Platform (GCP), Microsoft Azure: These cloud platforms provide scalable compute resources and machine learning services. They offer pre-configured environments for machine learning, making it easier to train and deploy models at scale.

7. Version Control

Git: Git is a widely used version control system that helps teams manage code changes efficiently. Platforms like GitHub and GitLab provide hosting and collaboration features for machine learning projects.

8. Collaboration Tools

Slack, Microsoft Teams: Communication tools like Slack and Microsoft Teams are essential for collaboration among team members working on machine learning projects. They facilitate discussions, file sharing, and project management.

9. Automated Machine Learning (AutoML) Tools

AutoML platforms: AutoML tools like Google AutoML, H2O.ai, and DataRobot automate various aspects of the machine learning workflow, including feature engineering, hyperparameter tuning, and model selection.

10. Model Deployment and Serving Tools

Docker and Kubernetes: These containerization and orchestration tools are commonly used for packaging and deploying machine learning models as containers.

Flask, FastAPI: These web frameworks are suitable for creating RESTful APIs to serve machine learning models in production.

11. Monitoring and Logging Tools

Prometheus, Grafana: These tools help monitor the performance and health of deployed machine learning models and infrastructure.

DATA PREPROCESSING

Data Collection and Acquisition

Data collection is the very first step in the journey of creating a successful machine learning model. The quality, quantity, and relevance of your data will greatly influence the effectiveness of your model.

The Importance of Quality Data

Imagine building a house on a shaky foundation—it might stand for a while, but it's bound to collapse eventually. The same principle applies to machine learning. Your model is only as good as the data it's trained on. Quality data is the sturdy foundation upon which your model's intelligence is built.

Here are some key reasons why quality data is essential:

1. **Accuracy**: High-quality data ensures that your model's predictions are accurate and reliable. If the data is riddled with errors or inaccuracies, your model will learn from those mistakes and make incorrect predictions.
2. **Generalization**: Quality data allows your model to generalize well to new, unseen data. If the training data is noisy or

unrepresentative of the problem you're trying to solve, your model will struggle to make accurate predictions in the real world.

3. **Bias Mitigation**: Biased data can lead to biased models, which can have significant ethical and fairness implications. Ensuring that your data is representative and free from bias is crucial, especially in applications that impact people's lives.

Data Collection Strategies

Data collection involves gathering data from various sources, and the strategies you employ depend on your project's goals and available resources. Here are some common strategies for data collection:

1. **Surveys and Questionnaires**: Surveys and questionnaires are useful for collecting structured data from human respondents. They are commonly used in social science research, marketing studies, and user feedback analysis.
2. **Web Scraping**: Web scraping is the process of extracting data from websites. It's often used to collect information from online sources such as news articles, e-commerce websites, or social media platforms.
3. **Sensor Data**: In IoT (Internet of Things) applications, data is collected from sensors embedded in devices. This data can include temperature readings, GPS coordinates, and more.
4. **APIs (Application Programming Interfaces)**: Many online services provide APIs that allow you to access and retrieve data programmatically. Examples include weather data from weather APIs, financial data from stock market APIs, and social media data from platforms like Twitter.
5. **Logs and Databases**: In business and IT, data is often collected through logs generated by applications, server activity, or user interactions. Databases store structured data that can be accessed for analysis.
6. **Image and Video Data**: Image and video data can be captured using cameras or collected from public sources. This type of data is essential for computer vision and multimedia analysis.

Data Privacy and Ethics

Collecting data comes with responsibilities, especially when dealing with personal or sensitive information. Data privacy and ethical considerations are crucial aspects of data collection. Ensure that you comply with relevant laws and regulations, such as GDPR (General Data Protection Regulation) in Europe, and prioritize user consent and data anonymization when necessary.

Data Acquisition Challenges

Data collection can present several challenges:

1. **Data Availability**: Sometimes, the data you need may not be readily available. You may need to negotiate with data providers or consider alternative sources.
2. **Data Quality**: Ensuring data quality, consistency, and accuracy can be time-consuming. Cleaning and preprocessing data are essential steps in addressing these challenges.
3. **Data Volume**: In some cases, you may need a large volume of data to train your model effectively. Managing and storing large datasets can be challenging.
4. **Bias and Fairness**: Carefully consider potential biases in your data and take steps to mitigate them. Biased data can lead to biased models and unfair predictions.

Data Cleaning

Data is often messy, inconsistent, and riddled with imperfections. Data cleaning, also known as data preprocessing or data wrangling, is the crucial process of transforming raw data into a clean and structured format suitable for analysis and modeling.

The Significance of Data Cleaning

Imagine trying to read a book with typos on every page, missing chapters, and pages in the wrong order. It would be a frustrating and nearly impossible task. Similarly, machine learning algorithms rely on clean and reliable data to learn patterns and make accurate predictions. Here's why data cleaning matters:

1. **Accuracy**: Clean data leads to more accurate model predictions. Data errors can propagate through the modeling process, causing inaccuracies in the final results.
2. **Consistency**: Consistent data ensures that your model interprets values and relationships correctly. Inconsistent data can confuse models and lead to misinterpretations.
3. **Robustness**: Clean data makes your model more robust. When presented with new, unseen data, a model trained on clean data is more likely to generalize well.

Common Data Quality Issues

Data quality issues can manifest in various forms, and it's essential to recognize and address them during the data cleaning process. Here are some common data quality issues:

1. **Missing Data**: Some data points may be missing entirely, which can lead to incomplete records and biased analyses if not handled properly.
2. **Outliers**: Outliers are data points that deviate significantly from the norm. They can skew statistical analyses and affect model performance.
3. **Inconsistent Formatting**: Data may be stored in different formats or units, making it challenging to compare and analyze.
4. **Duplicates**: Duplicate records can lead to overrepresentation of certain data points, potentially biasing your analysis.
5. **Incorrect Values**: Data may contain incorrect or unrealistic values that need to be corrected or removed.
6. **Categorical Data Encoding**: Categorical variables often need to be properly encoded for machine learning models to understand them.

Data Cleaning Techniques

Data cleaning involves a series of techniques and strategies to address data quality issues. Here are some essential data cleaning techniques:

1. **Handling Missing Data**: Missing data can be imputed (filled in) using techniques such as mean, median, or mode imputation. In some cases, it may be appropriate to drop rows or columns with a high proportion of missing values.
2. **Outlier Detection and Handling**: Outliers can be detected using statistical methods or visualization techniques. Depending on the context, outliers can be corrected, removed, or treated separately in the analysis.
3. **Data Transformation**: Data may need to be transformed to achieve consistency. This can include converting units, normalizing values, or applying mathematical functions to achieve a common scale.
4. **Deduplication**: Identifying and removing duplicate records can improve the quality of your dataset.
5. **Encoding Categorical Data**: Categorical variables are often encoded using techniques like one-hot encoding or label encoding to make them suitable for machine learning models.
6. **Data Validation**: Implement data validation checks to ensure that values fall within expected ranges and that relationships between variables make sense.
7. **Feature Engineering**: Creating new features or modifying existing ones can improve model performance. This can involve combining, aggregating, or transforming features to capture meaningful patterns.
8. **Data Visualization**: Data visualization can help identify data quality issues and provide insights into the data. Tools like scatter plots, histograms, and box plots are valuable for visual data inspection.

Iterative Process

Data cleaning is often an iterative process. After applying initial cleaning techniques, it's essential to assess the impact on your data and continue refining the process as needed. Cleaning may reveal further issues that were not initially apparent.

Data Exploration and Visualization

Data exploration and visualization are indispensable steps in the data analysis and machine learning process. They provide insights into the underlying structure of your data, reveal patterns and trends, and help you make informed decisions about feature engineering, model selection, and data preprocessing.

The Importance of Data Exploration

Data exploration serves several crucial purposes:

1. **Understanding the Data**: Exploring your dataset helps you understand its characteristics, including the distribution of features, the presence of outliers, and the relationships between variables.
2. **Identifying Data Quality Issues**: Data exploration can reveal data quality issues such as missing values, outliers, or inconsistencies that need to be addressed during data preprocessing.
3. **Feature Selection and Engineering**: Through exploration, you can identify which features are most relevant for your task and potentially create new features that capture meaningful patterns.
4. **Model Selection**: Visualization aids in choosing appropriate machine learning algorithms by highlighting the nature of the data and the problem. Different algorithms may be better suited to different data distributions.
5. **Communication**: Visualizations are an effective way to communicate your findings and insights to stakeholders, team members, or non-technical audiences.

Data Exploration Techniques

Here are some essential techniques for data exploration:

1. **Summary Statistics**: Start with basic summary statistics like mean, median, standard deviation, and percentiles to get a sense of the central tendency and spread of your data.
2. **Data Distribution**: Visualize data distributions using histograms, density plots, or box plots to understand the shape and spread of each feature.
3. **Correlation Analysis**: Examine correlations between features to identify relationships. Correlation matrices and scatter plots are useful for this purpose.
4. **Pairwise Comparisons**: Compare pairs of features to understand how they interact. Scatter plots and two-dimensional histograms can reveal interesting patterns.
5. **Time Series Analysis**: If your data involves time-dependent variables, time series analysis can help you uncover trends and seasonality patterns.
6. **Dimensionality Reduction**: Techniques like Principal Component Analysis (PCA) or t-SNE (t-Distributed Stochastic Neighbor Embedding) can reduce the dimensionality of your data while preserving essential information for visualization.

Data Visualization Tools

Various tools and libraries are available for data visualization:

1. **Matplotlib**: Matplotlib is a versatile Python library for creating static, animated, and interactive visualizations. It's highly customizable and widely used for data exploration.
2. **Seaborn**: Seaborn is built on top of Matplotlib and provides a high-level interface for creating attractive and informative statistical graphics.
3. **Plotly**: Plotly is known for its interactive and web-based visualizations. It supports a wide range of chart types and can be embedded in web applications.
4. **ggplot2**: ggplot2 is a popular R package for creating elegant and expressive data visualizations, particularly for those familiar with the grammar of graphics.

5. **Tableau, Power BI**: These commercial tools offer user-friendly interfaces for creating interactive data dashboards and visualizations.

Interpreting Visualizations

When interpreting visualizations, consider the following questions:

- What do the patterns and trends in the data tell you about the problem?
- Are there any outliers or anomalies that need further investigation?
- Do the visualizations reveal relationships or correlations between variables?
- Are there clusters or groups within the data that suggest distinct patterns?
- Do the visualizations suggest any potential feature engineering opportunities?

Remember that data exploration and visualization are iterative processes. As you gain insights and make decisions about data preprocessing and model selection, you may return to the exploration phase to refine your understanding of the data.

Feature Engineering

Feature engineering is an art as much as it is a science in the realm of data science and machine learning. It involves crafting and transforming raw data into meaningful, informative, and predictive features that enhance the performance of machine learning models.

The Importance of Feature Engineering

Why is feature engineering so crucial in the machine learning workflow? Here's why:

1. **Improved Model Performance**: Well-engineered features can significantly boost a model's predictive power. They can help models capture complex relationships, reduce overfitting, and enhance generalization to unseen data.
2. **Relevance**: Feature engineering allows you to focus on the most relevant aspects of your data, discarding irrelevant or redundant information that might confuse the model.
3. **Interpretability**: Engineered features can make your model's predictions more interpretable and understandable, which is vital in applications where transparency is important.
4. **Domain Knowledge**: Feature engineering often requires domain expertise. It's an opportunity to inject domain-specific knowledge into your model, making it more attuned to the problem you're solving.

Common Feature Engineering Techniques

Feature engineering involves a myriad of techniques, depending on the nature of the data and the problem you're tackling. Here are some common feature engineering techniques:

1. **Handling Missing Values**: Create new features to indicate whether a value is missing in a specific column. This can help the model distinguish between cases where data is available and where it's not.
2. **Binning and Bucketing**: Transform continuous features into categorical ones by grouping values into bins or buckets. This can help capture non-linear relationships.
3. **One-Hot Encoding**: Convert categorical variables into binary columns, each representing a category. This enables the model to work with categorical data.
4. **Feature Scaling**: Standardize or normalize numerical features to ensure they have a similar scale. This can improve the performance of models that rely on distance-based metrics.
5. **Logarithmic and Power Transformations**: Apply logarithmic or power transformations to features to make their distributions more Gaussian-like, which can be beneficial for some algorithms.

6. **Feature Crosses**: Create new features by combining existing ones. For example, you might multiply the "length" and "width" features to capture the notion of area in a dataset of geometric shapes.
7. **Text Vectorization**: Convert text data into numerical representations using techniques like TF-IDF (Term Frequency-Inverse Document Frequency) or word embeddings like Word2Vec or GloVe.
8. **Date and Time Features**: Extract information like day of the week, month, or time of day from date and time variables. These features can be valuable in time-series analysis.
9. **Aggregation**: Aggregate data over different groups or time periods. For instance, you might calculate the mean or sum of a numerical feature within specific categories.
10. **Interaction Features**: Create features that capture interactions between variables. For example, in a recommendation system, you might create a feature that represents the user's historical preference for a particular genre of movies.

Feature Engineering Best Practices

When performing feature engineering, keep these best practices in mind:

1. **Domain Knowledge**: Understand the domain of your problem. Domain-specific knowledge can guide you in selecting relevant features and creating meaningful transformations.
2. **Iterate and Experiment**: Feature engineering is often an iterative process. Don't hesitate to try various techniques, test their impact on model performance, and refine your feature engineering strategy accordingly.
3. **Feature Importance**: Use techniques like feature importance scores to identify which features are most influential in your model's predictions. This can guide your feature engineering efforts.
4. **Avoid Data Leakage**: Be cautious to prevent data leakage, where information from the target variable inadvertently

finds its way into the features. This can lead to overly optimistic model evaluations.

5. **Documentation**: Keep detailed documentation of your feature engineering steps. This helps ensure reproducibility and allows you to communicate your work effectively to others.

Feature engineering is both a creative and analytical process that bridges the gap between raw data and machine learning models. It's a skill that evolves with experience and domain expertise. When done effectively, feature engineering can turn a good model into a great one, unlocking the full potential of your data and advancing the state of the art in your machine learning projects.

Data Scaling and Normalization

Data in real-world applications often comes in various units and scales, making it challenging for machine learning algorithms to work effectively. Data scaling and normalization are preprocessing techniques used to transform and standardize numerical features, ensuring that they are on a consistent scale.

Why Data Scaling and Normalization Matter

The scales and units of numerical features can vary widely in a dataset. For example, consider a dataset containing both house prices in dollars and the number of bedrooms. The price values could be in the thousands or millions, while the number of bedrooms typically ranges from 1 to 5. Here's why scaling and normalization are important:

1. **Equal Treatment**: Scaling ensures that all features are treated equally by machine learning algorithms. Without scaling, features with larger scales can dominate the learning process.
2. **Improved Convergence**: Scaling can lead to faster convergence during model training. Algorithms that rely on

distance metrics (e.g., k-means clustering, support vector machines) can benefit significantly from scaled data.

3. **Model Performance**: Scaling can improve the performance of certain machine learning algorithms, particularly those sensitive to the scale of input data, like gradient descent-based optimization algorithms used in neural networks.

Common Scaling and Normalization Techniques

Here are some common techniques for scaling and normalization:

1. **Min-Max Scaling (Normalization)**:
   - Also known as min-max normalization, this method scales features to a specific range, typically between 0 and 1.
   - The formula for min-max scaling is: $X_{normalized} = (X - X_{min}) / (X_{max} - X_{min})$
   - This technique is suitable when you want to preserve the relative relationships between feature values but ensure they are within a specific range.

2. **Z-Score Standardization (Standard Scaling)**:
   - Standardization transforms data to have a mean of 0 and a standard deviation of 1.
   - The formula for standardization is: $X_{standardized} = (X - X_{mean}) / X_{stddev}$
   - It is appropriate when you want to center the data around zero and rescale it, making it suitable for algorithms that assume Gaussian (normal) distributions.

3. **Robust Scaling**:
   - Robust scaling is a technique that scales features using robust statistics, making it resistant to the influence of outliers.
   - It uses the median and interquartile range (IQR) instead of the mean and standard deviation.
   - This method is a good choice when your data contains outliers that can skew the scaling.

4. **Log Transformation**:

- o Logarithmic transformation can be used when data has a skewed distribution.
- o Applying a logarithmic function can make the distribution more symmetrical and alleviate the impact of extreme values.

5. **Power Transformation**:
   - o Power transformations, such as the Box-Cox and Yeo-Johnson transformations, can be applied to stabilize variance and make data more Gaussian-like.

Choosing the Right Technique

The choice of scaling or normalization technique depends on the nature of your data and the requirements of your machine learning algorithm. Min-max scaling and standardization are commonly used, but it's essential to consider the characteristics of your data, including the presence of outliers, before deciding on the most appropriate method.

Scaling in Practice

When performing data scaling and normalization, it's crucial to fit any scalers or transformers on the training data and then apply them consistently to both the training and testing datasets. This ensures that the scaling parameters are not influenced by the test data, preventing data leakage.

SUPERVISED LEARNING

Introduction to Supervised Learning

What Is Supervised Learning?

Supervised learning is one of the core branches of machine learning, and it's all about teaching machines to make predictions or classify data based on a set of labeled examples. These labeled examples consist of input data paired with corresponding target labels, effectively providing the machine with a roadmap for learning. The goal is for the machine to generalize from the labeled examples and make accurate predictions or classifications on new, unseen data.

Here's a breakdown of the key components:

- **Input Data**: This is the raw data that the machine uses to learn patterns and relationships. It can take various forms, such as images, text, numerical values, or a combination of these.
- **Target Labels**: Target labels are the correct answers or categories associated with the input data. They represent the desired outcomes that the machine aims to predict or classify.
- **Training**: During the training phase, the machine uses the labeled examples to learn patterns and build a predictive or

classification model. It analyzes the input data and adjusts its internal parameters to minimize the difference between its predictions and the true target labels.

- **Testing and Inference**: After training, the machine is put to the test with new, unseen data. It uses the learned model to make predictions or classifications on this test data, allowing us to evaluate its performance.

Regression vs. Classification

In supervised learning, tasks typically fall into one of two categories: regression or classification.

- **Regression**: In regression tasks, the goal is to predict a continuous numerical value. For example, predicting house prices based on features like square footage, number of bedrooms, and location is a regression problem.
- **Classification**: In classification tasks, the goal is to assign data points to predefined categories or classes. Examples include spam email detection (classifying emails as spam or not) and image recognition (identifying objects in images).

Applications of Supervised Learning

Supervised learning is a versatile and powerful tool with a wide range of applications across various domains. Some notable examples include:

- **Medical Diagnosis**: Predicting disease outcomes based on patient data and medical records.
- **Natural Language Processing (NLP)**: Classifying documents, sentiment analysis, and machine translation.
- **Recommendation Systems**: Recommending products, movies, or content based on user preferences.
- **Financial Forecasting**: Predicting stock prices, credit risk assessment, and fraud detection.
- **Image and Video Analysis**: Object detection, facial recognition, and autonomous vehicle perception.

Linear Regression

Linear regression is one of the fundamental algorithms in machine learning and statistics. It's a powerful tool for modeling the relationship between a dependent variable (often called the target or response) and one or more independent variables (predictors or features). This technique is widely used for tasks such as predicting sales, analyzing trends, and understanding the relationship between variables in various fields, including economics, biology, and social sciences.

Understanding Linear Regression

At its core, linear regression aims to find the best-fit linear equation that describes the relationship between the independent variables and the dependent variable. The equation for a simple linear regression model with one independent variable looks like this:

$$Y = \beta 0 + \beta 1 X + \square$$

Where:

- Y is the dependent variable we want to predict.
- X is the independent variable or feature.
- $\beta 0$ is the intercept (the value of Y when X is 0).
- $\beta 1$ is the slope, representing how much Y changes for a one-unit change in X.
- $\square$ represents the error term, accounting for the variability in Y that is not explained by the linear relationship with X.

In simple terms, linear regression tries to find the values of $\beta 0$ and $\beta 1$ that minimize the sum of squared differences between the predicted values and the actual values in the training data. This process is often referred to as "fitting" the model.

Types of Linear Regression

There are two main types of linear regression:

1. **Simple Linear Regression**: This type involves a single independent variable. It's suitable for modeling relationships between two variables, such as predicting a person's weight based on their height.
2. **Multiple Linear Regression**: In this case, there are two or more independent variables, allowing you to model more complex relationships. For example, you might predict a house's price based on features like square footage, number of bedrooms, and neighborhood.

Assumptions of Linear Regression

Linear regression makes several assumptions about the data:

1. **Linearity**: The relationship between the independent and dependent variables is assumed to be linear.
2. **Independence**: The observations or data points are assumed to be independent of each other.
3. **Homoscedasticity**: The variance of the error terms is constant across all levels of the independent variables.
4. **Normality**: The error terms are normally distributed.
5. **No or Little Multicollinearity**: The independent variables are not highly correlated with each other.

Applications of Linear Regression

Linear regression has a wide range of applications, including:

- **Sales Forecasting**: Predicting future sales based on historical data and marketing efforts.
- **Economic Analysis**: Modeling the relationship between factors like GDP and unemployment rates.
- **Medical Research**: Predicting patient outcomes based on medical data.
- **Climate Science**: Analyzing the relationship between temperature and greenhouse gas emissions.

- **Education**: Predicting student performance based on various factors like study time and attendance.

Challenges and Limitations

While linear regression is a powerful and interpretable technique, it has its limitations. For instance, it assumes a linear relationship between variables, which may not always hold in real-world scenarios. Additionally, it's sensitive to outliers and can be influenced by the choice of independent variables.

Logistic Regression

Logistic regression is a widely used statistical and machine learning technique for binary and multiclass classification problems. Despite its name, logistic regression is primarily used for classification rather than regression tasks. It's a powerful tool for modeling the probability of an event occurring based on one or more predictor variables.

Understanding Logistic Regression

Unlike linear regression, which predicts continuous numeric values, logistic regression predicts the probability that an input belongs to a particular class. The output of logistic regression is a probability score between 0 and 1, which can be interpreted as the likelihood of the input belonging to the positive class (typically denoted as class 1).

Multiclass Logistic Regression

Logistic regression can be extended to handle multiclass classification problems. In this scenario, the model predicts the probabilities for each class, and the class with the highest probability is chosen as the final prediction. One common approach for multiclass logistic regression is the "one-vs-all" (or "one-vs-rest") strategy, where a separate binary logistic regression model is trained for each class.

Applications of Logistic Regression

Logistic regression finds applications in a wide range of fields, including:

- **Medical Diagnosis**: Predicting whether a patient has a disease based on medical test results.
- **Credit Scoring**: Assessing the creditworthiness of individuals based on financial and personal data.
- **Marketing**: Predicting whether a customer will purchase a product or churn from a service.
- **Natural Language Processing (NLP)**: Text classification tasks like sentiment analysis and spam detection.
- **Image Recognition**: Multiclass classification of objects in images.
- **Quality Control**: Identifying defective products in manufacturing.

Advantages and Limitations

Advantages of logistic regression include:

- Simplicity and interpretability: Logistic regression models are relatively easy to interpret, making them valuable for understanding the relationship between features and the target variable.
- Efficiency: Logistic regression can handle large datasets efficiently and can be trained quickly.
- Low risk of overfitting: Logistic regression is less prone to overfitting compared to more complex models.

Limitations of logistic regression include:

- Linearity assumption: Logistic regression assumes a linear relationship between the input features and the log-odds of the target variable, which may not hold for all problems.
- Limited expressiveness: Logistic regression may not capture complex nonlinear relationships in the data as effectively as more complex models.

- Vulnerability to outliers: Extreme outliers can have a significant impact on logistic regression models.

Decision Trees and Random Forests

Decision trees and random forests are versatile machine learning techniques used for both classification and regression tasks. These algorithms are known for their simplicity, interpretability, and ability to handle complex data relationships.

Decision Trees

A decision tree is a hierarchical structure that resembles a tree, where each internal node represents a decision or test on a feature, each branch represents an outcome of the test, and each leaf node represents a class label (in classification) or a numeric value (in regression). Decision trees are constructed through a recursive process called "tree induction," which involves selecting the best feature to split the data based on certain criteria, such as information gain or Gini impurity.

Key characteristics of decision trees:

- **Interpretability**: Decision trees provide a straightforward way to visualize and interpret the decision-making process, making them valuable for explaining model predictions.
- **Non-linearity**: Decision trees can capture complex non-linear relationships in the data.
- **Overfitting**: Decision trees are prone to overfitting when they become too deep or complex. Overfit trees fit the training data perfectly but may perform poorly on unseen data.
- **Instability**: Small changes in the training data can lead to significant changes in the tree structure, making decision trees somewhat unstable.

Random Forests

Random forests are an ensemble learning method that builds multiple decision trees and combines their predictions to improve overall accuracy and reduce overfitting. The "random" part in random forests comes from two sources:

1. **Bootstrapped Data**: Each tree in the random forest is trained on a randomly selected subset of the training data. This process, known as bootstrapping, introduces diversity into the training process.
2. **Feature Subsampling**: When considering a feature to split a node, random forests randomly select a subset of features from which to choose. This helps in decorrelating the trees and reducing model variance.

Key characteristics of random forests:

- **Reduced Overfitting**: By averaging the predictions of multiple trees, random forests are less prone to overfitting compared to individual decision trees.
- **Improved Generalization**: Random forests tend to generalize well to unseen data, making them robust and reliable.
- **Feature Importance**: Random forests can provide insights into feature importance, helping identify which features are most influential in making predictions.
- **Scalability**: Random forests can handle large datasets and high-dimensional feature spaces.

Applications of Decision Trees and Random Forests

Decision trees and random forests find applications in various domains, including:

- **Healthcare**: Predicting disease outcomes based on patient data and medical records.
- **Finance**: Assessing credit risk, detecting fraudulent transactions, and forecasting stock prices.
- **Marketing**: Identifying customer segments and predicting purchase behavior.

- **Environmental Science**: Classifying species based on environmental variables.
- **Image Analysis**: Object detection and image classification tasks.
- **Anomaly Detection**: Identifying anomalies in data, such as network intrusion detection.

Advantages and Limitations

Advantages of decision trees and random forests:

- **Interpretability**: Decision trees are easy to visualize and interpret. Random forests, while more complex, can still provide insights into feature importance.
- **Versatility**: These algorithms can handle both categorical and numerical data.
- **Robustness**: Random forests are less sensitive to outliers and noisy data compared to some other algorithms.
- **Ensemble Benefits**: Random forests improve upon the limitations of individual decision trees.

Limitations:

- **Complexity**: Individual decision trees can become overly complex and prone to overfitting, while random forests may require more computational resources.
- **Loss of Transparency**: As random forests combine multiple trees, they may lose some of the interpretability inherent in single decision trees.
- **Parameter Tuning**: Fine-tuning hyperparameters for random forests can be challenging.

Support Vector Machines (SVMs)

Support Vector Machines (SVMs) are a versatile and powerful class of machine learning algorithms used for both classification and regression tasks. SVMs are particularly well-suited for scenarios where the data is not linearly separable, meaning there is no straight line (in 2D) or hyperplane (in higher dimensions) that can perfectly separate the data points of different classes. SVMs can handle such cases by finding the optimal separating hyperplane while maximizing the margin between classes.

The Intuition Behind SVMs

The fundamental idea behind SVMs can be understood by considering the concept of a margin. The margin is the distance between the separating hyperplane and the nearest data points of each class. In SVMs, the goal is to find the hyperplane that maximizes this margin while ensuring that it correctly classifies as many data points as possible.

Key concepts related to SVMs:

1. **Hyperplane**: In a two-dimensional space, a hyperplane is a straight line. In higher dimensions, it's a flat affine subspace. For classification, SVMs aim to find the hyperplane that best separates the classes.
2. **Support Vectors**: These are the data points closest to the hyperplane and are crucial in determining the position and orientation of the hyperplane.
3. **Margin**: The margin is the perpendicular distance from the support vectors to the hyperplane. SVMs aim to maximize this margin.

Linear SVM

In its simplest form, SVMs are used for linearly separable data. The decision boundary (hyperplane) is chosen such that it maximizes the margin between the classes. The mathematical representation of a linear SVM is as follows:

Decision Function: $f(x) = \text{sign}(w \cdot x + b)$

Where:

- f(x) is the decision function that predicts the class label for a new data point xx.
- w is the weight vector that determines the orientation of the hyperplane.
- x represents the input features.
- b is the bias term, which shifts the hyperplane away from the origin.

Non-Linear SVM (Kernel SVM)

In many real-world scenarios, data is not linearly separable. SVMs can handle this by using kernel functions, which implicitly map the input data into a higher-dimensional space where it becomes linearly separable. Common kernel functions include:

- **Linear Kernel**: Suitable for linearly separable data.
- **Polynomial Kernel**: Appropriate for data with complex polynomial boundaries.
- **Radial Basis Function (RBF) Kernel**: Effective for data with non-linear, complex decision boundaries.

Choosing the right kernel and tuning its parameters is crucial for achieving good SVM performance.

Applications of SVMs

Support Vector Machines have a wide range of applications, including:

- **Image Classification**: Recognizing objects and patterns in images.
- **Text Classification**: Categorizing text documents into topics or sentiment analysis.
- **Handwriting Recognition**: Identifying handwritten characters or words.
- **Biomedical Research**: Identifying disease biomarkers or protein classification.
- **Anomaly Detection**: Detecting anomalies or fraud in financial transactions.

- **Face Detection**: Identifying faces in images or videos.

Advantages and Limitations

Advantages of SVMs:

- **Effective in High-Dimensional Spaces**: SVMs perform well even in high-dimensional feature spaces, making them suitable for complex data.
- **Robust to Overfitting**: SVMs are less prone to overfitting compared to some other algorithms, thanks to the margin concept.
- **Kernel Flexibility**: The ability to use various kernel functions allows SVMs to capture complex data relationships.

Limitations:

- **Computational Complexity**: Training SVMs can be computationally expensive, especially with large datasets.
- **Choice of Kernel**: Selecting the right kernel and tuning its parameters can be challenging.
- **Interpretability**: SVMs may not be as interpretable as simpler models like decision trees or linear regression.

K-Nearest Neighbors (KNN)

K-Nearest Neighbors, often abbreviated as KNN, is a simple and intuitive machine learning algorithm used for classification and regression tasks. It's a non-parametric, instance-based learning method that makes predictions based on the similarity between new data points and existing data points in a labeled dataset. KNN is easy to understand and implement, making it a valuable tool in various applications.

The Intuition Behind KNN

The fundamental idea behind KNN is that similar data points tend to belong to the same class or have similar target values. KNN makes predictions by looking at the K-nearest data points to the new data point in question. In classification, the majority class among the K-nearest neighbors is assigned as the predicted class. In regression, the average (or another aggregation) of the K-nearest neighbors' target values is used as the prediction.

Key Concepts in KNN:

1. **K**: K represents the number of nearest neighbors to consider when making predictions. Choosing an appropriate value for K is essential. A smaller K may lead to a noisy prediction, while a larger K may result in a smoother but potentially biased prediction.
2. **Distance Metric**: To measure similarity, a distance metric, such as Euclidean distance or Manhattan distance, is used to calculate the distances between data points.
3. **Majority Voting (Classification)**: For classification tasks, the class label that appears most frequently among the K-nearest neighbors is assigned as the predicted class.
4. **Average (Regression)**: For regression tasks, the average (or weighted average) of the K-nearest neighbors' target values is used as the prediction.

KNN in Action: Classification

Here's a simplified example of KNN in a classification scenario:

1. You have a dataset with labeled data points, each belonging to one of two classes: "Red" or "Blue."
2. You want to predict the class of a new data point (represented by a star on a graph).
3. To make this prediction, KNN calculates the distance between the star and its K-nearest neighbors from the dataset.
4. If, for example, the majority of the K-nearest neighbors are "Red," the star would be classified as "Red."

KNN in Action: Regression

In a regression scenario, KNN works similarly but predicts a numeric value instead of a class label. For instance, it could predict the price of a house based on the prices of its K-nearest neighbor houses.

Applications of KNN

KNN has a wide range of applications, including:

- **Recommendation Systems**: Recommending products or content based on user behavior and preferences.
- **Image Recognition**: Identifying objects in images by comparing them to a database of labeled images.
- **Anomaly Detection**: Detecting unusual patterns or outliers in data.
- **Predictive Maintenance**: Predicting when equipment or machines might fail based on historical data.
- **Medical Diagnosis**: Identifying diseases or conditions based on patient data and medical records.

Advantages and Limitations

Advantages of KNN:

- **Simplicity**: KNN is easy to understand and implement, making it a good choice for quick prototyping.
- **Flexibility**: KNN can be used for both classification and regression tasks.
- **No Training Phase**: KNN does not require an explicit training phase; it memorizes the entire dataset.

Limitations:

- **Computational Complexity**: KNN can be slow and computationally expensive, especially with large datasets or high dimensions.
- **Sensitivity to Noise**: KNN is sensitive to noisy data and outliers, which can lead to incorrect predictions.

- **Choosing K**: Selecting the right value for K can be challenging and can significantly impact the algorithm's performance.

Model Evaluation and Metrics

Machine learning models are built to make predictions or classifications based on data. However, building a model is only part of the process; assessing its performance is equally important. Model evaluation involves measuring how well a model generalizes to new, unseen data and whether it meets the desired objectives. To perform this assessment, various evaluation metrics and techniques are used.

Why Model Evaluation Matters

Effective model evaluation serves several crucial purposes:

1. **Quality Assurance**: It ensures that the model's predictions align with the real-world outcomes you aim to predict.
2. **Comparison**: It allows you to compare different models to determine which one performs better on a specific task.
3. **Hyperparameter Tuning**: Model evaluation helps in fine-tuning hyperparameters to optimize a model's performance.
4. **Understanding Model Behavior**: It provides insights into a model's strengths and weaknesses, helping you identify areas for improvement.

Common Model Evaluation Metrics

The choice of evaluation metrics depends on the type of machine learning task, such as classification, regression, or clustering. Here are some commonly used metrics for different tasks:

Classification Metrics:

1. **Accuracy**: The proportion of correctly predicted instances out of the total instances. It's suitable when the class

distribution is balanced but can be misleading when classes are imbalanced.

2. **Precision**: The proportion of true positive predictions out of all positive predictions. It measures the model's ability to avoid false positives.

3. **Recall (Sensitivity)**: The proportion of true positive predictions out of all actual positives. It quantifies the model's ability to capture positive instances.

4. **F1-Score**: The harmonic mean of precision and recall. It provides a balanced measure of a model's performance.

5. **ROC Curve and AUC**: Receiver Operating Characteristic (ROC) curves plot the trade-off between true positive rate (recall) and false positive rate at different thresholds. The Area Under the ROC Curve (AUC) quantifies the overall performance of the model.

6. **Confusion Matrix**: A table that summarizes the true positive, true negative, false positive, and false negative predictions.

Regression Metrics:

1. **Mean Absolute Error (MAE)**: The average absolute difference between predicted and actual values. It's easy to interpret but not very robust to outliers.

2. **Mean Squared Error (MSE)**: The average squared difference between predicted and actual values. It amplifies the impact of outliers.

3. **Root Mean Squared Error (RMSE)**: The square root of MSE. It has the same units as the target variable, making it easier to interpret.

4. **R-squared (R²)**: A measure of how well the model explains the variance in the target variable. It ranges from 0 to 1, with higher values indicating a better fit.

Clustering Metrics:

1. **Silhouette Score**: Measures how similar an object is to its cluster compared to other clusters. Higher values indicate better cluster quality.

2. **Inertia**: The sum of squared distances between data points and their cluster centroids. It helps assess the compactness of clusters.

Cross-Validation

Cross-validation is a crucial technique for model evaluation. It involves splitting the data into multiple subsets (folds), training the model on some folds, and evaluating it on others. Common cross-validation methods include k-fold cross-validation and stratified k-fold cross-validation.

Bias-Variance Trade-Off

Understanding the bias-variance trade-off is essential for model evaluation. High bias (underfitting) indicates that the model is too simple to capture the data's complexity. High variance (overfitting) suggests that the model is too complex and captures noise. Achieving a balance between bias and variance leads to a model that generalizes well to new data.

UNSUPERVISED LEARNING

Clustering Algorithms: K-Means and Hierarchical Clustering

Clustering is the process of grouping similar data points together based on their inherent characteristics or patterns. It's a fundamental unsupervised learning technique that finds applications across various domains, including data analysis, customer segmentation, image recognition, and more. Two of the most widely used clustering algorithms are K-Means and Hierarchical Clustering.

K-Means Clustering

K-Means: Dividing Data into K Clusters

K-Means is a popular and efficient clustering algorithm that aims to partition a dataset into K distinct, non-overlapping clusters. The primary idea behind K-Means is to group data points into clusters by minimizing the sum of squared distances between data points within the same cluster and the cluster's centroid (the center point of the cluster).

How K-Means Works:

1. **Initialization**: The algorithm starts by selecting K initial centroids, typically randomly chosen from the data points or using other initialization techniques.
2. **Assignment**: Each data point is assigned to the nearest centroid, forming K clusters.
3. **Update Centroids**: The centroids of the clusters are recalculated as the mean (average) of all data points assigned to that cluster.
4. **Re-Assignment and Update**: Steps 2 and 3 are repeated iteratively until the centroids no longer change significantly, or a predefined number of iterations is reached.

Advantages of K-Means:

- **Efficiency**: K-Means is computationally efficient and can handle large datasets.
- **Scalability**: It scales well with the number of data points and clusters.
- **Ease of Interpretation**: K-Means results in easily interpretable clusters.

Limitations of K-Means:

- **Dependent on Initial Centroids**: The algorithm's performance can be sensitive to the choice of initial centroids.
- **Assumes Spherical Clusters**: K-Means works well when clusters are spherical and equally sized, which may not always be the case in real data.
- **May Converge to Local Optima**: K-Means can converge to a suboptimal solution depending on the initial centroids.

Hierarchical Clustering

Hierarchical Clustering: Building a Tree of Clusters

Hierarchical Clustering, as the name suggests, builds a hierarchy of clusters. It doesn't require specifying the number of clusters (K) beforehand, making it a valuable technique when you're unsure about the ideal cluster count. Hierarchical Clustering methods create a tree-like structure called a dendrogram, which visually represents the clustering process.

How Hierarchical Clustering Works:

1. **Initialization**: Each data point starts as its own cluster, and the algorithm proceeds to merge clusters iteratively.
2. **Merge Criteria**: Clusters are merged based on a specified linkage criterion, which defines the distance between clusters. Common linkage criteria include:
   - **Single Linkage**: Minimum distance between data points in two clusters.
   - **Complete Linkage**: Maximum distance between data points in two clusters.
   - **Average Linkage**: Average distance between data points in two clusters.
3. **Dendrogram Creation**: The algorithm builds a dendrogram that visually represents the hierarchy of clusters. The height of the dendrogram's branches represents the distance at which clusters were merged.
4. **Cutting the Dendrogram**: Based on your desired number of clusters or a threshold distance, you can cut the dendrogram to obtain the final clusters.

Advantages of Hierarchical Clustering:

- **No Predefined K**: Hierarchical Clustering does not require specifying the number of clusters beforehand.
- **Interpretability**: The dendrogram provides insights into the hierarchy of clustering.
- **Robustness**: It can handle different cluster shapes and sizes.

Limitations of Hierarchical Clustering:

- **Computational Complexity**: Hierarchical Clustering can be computationally expensive, especially with large datasets.
- **Non-Reproducibility**: The results can vary depending on the chosen linkage criterion and distance metric.

- **Difficulty in Choosing Cuts**: Deciding where to cut the dendrogram to obtain the final clusters can be subjective.

Choosing Between K-Means and Hierarchical Clustering:

The choice between K-Means and Hierarchical Clustering depends on factors such as the nature of your data, the desired number of clusters, and the interpretability of the results. K-Means is efficient and suitable for a known number of clusters, while Hierarchical Clustering is versatile and can handle an unknown number of clusters.

Dimensionality Reduction: PCA and t-SNE

Dimensionality reduction is a fundamental technique in machine learning and data analysis that involves reducing the number of features or variables in a dataset while preserving its essential structure and patterns. It is used to tackle problems associated with high-dimensional data, such as the curse of dimensionality, computational complexity, and overfitting. Two commonly used dimensionality reduction techniques are Principal Component Analysis (PCA) and t-Distributed Stochastic Neighbor Embedding (t-SNE).

Principal Component Analysis (PCA)

PCA: Transforming Dimensions into Principal Components

Principal Component Analysis (PCA) is a linear dimensionality reduction technique that transforms high-dimensional data into a lower-dimensional space. It does this by finding the principal components, which are linear combinations of the original features that capture the maximum variance in the data. These principal components are orthogonal to each other, meaning they are uncorrelated.

How PCA Works:

1. **Standardization**: PCA often starts by standardizing the data to have zero mean and unit variance.
2. **Covariance Matrix**: It computes the covariance matrix of the standardized data, representing the relationships between features.
3. **Eigenvalue Decomposition**: PCA then performs eigenvalue decomposition on the covariance matrix to find its eigenvalues and eigenvectors.
4. **Selecting Principal Components**: The eigenvectors with the highest eigenvalues correspond to the principal components. By selecting a subset of these components, you can reduce the dimensionality while retaining most of the variance in the data.
5. **Projection**: Finally, the data is projected onto the selected principal components to obtain the reduced-dimensional representation.

Advantages of PCA:

- **Dimension Reduction**: PCA is effective in reducing the dimensionality of data, making it more manageable.
- **Decorrelation**: It produces uncorrelated principal components, which can be beneficial for downstream tasks.
- **Noise Reduction**: PCA can help remove noise and emphasize the most informative features.

Limitations of PCA:

- **Linearity**: PCA is a linear technique and may not capture complex non-linear relationships in the data.
- **Interpretability**: The principal components themselves may not be easily interpretable in terms of the original features.

t-Distributed Stochastic Neighbor Embedding (t-SNE)

t-SNE: Preserving Local and Global Structure

t-Distributed Stochastic Neighbor Embedding (t-SNE) is a nonlinear dimensionality reduction technique that focuses on preserving the similarity between data points. Unlike PCA, which emphasizes global patterns and variance, t-SNE aims to maintain the local structure of data, making it particularly useful for visualization and exploring complex data relationships.

How t-SNE Works:

1. **Similarity Measurement**: t-SNE calculates pairwise similarities between data points in the high-dimensional space, typically using a Gaussian distribution to measure similarities.
2. **Similarity Measurement in Low-Dimensional Space**: It also calculates pairwise similarities in a lower-dimensional space, initially random.
3. **Optimization**: t-SNE iteratively adjusts the positions of data points in the lower-dimensional space to minimize the difference between the two sets of pairwise similarities.
4. **Preservation of Clusters**: The algorithm encourages the preservation of clusters of similar data points and tends to push dissimilar points farther apart.

Advantages of t-SNE:

- **Local Structure Preservation**: t-SNE excels at preserving local relationships and clusters in data.
- **Visualization**: It is widely used for visualizing high-dimensional data in lower dimensions, aiding in data exploration.

Limitations of t-SNE:

- **Stochastic Nature**: t-SNE is stochastic, meaning it can produce different results on different runs with the same data.
- **Nonlinear**: It's a nonlinear technique, which can make it less suitable for certain tasks, such as linear classification.

Choosing Between PCA and t-SNE:

The choice between PCA and t-SNE depends on your specific goals. If you need to reduce dimensionality while preserving global patterns and variance, PCA is a solid choice. On the other hand, if you want to visualize data or preserve local structures and clusters, t-SNE is often preferred.

Anomaly Detection

Anomalies, also known as outliers or novelties, represent data points or patterns that differ significantly from the majority of data points in a dataset. Anomaly detection plays a vital role in various domains, including fraud detection, network security, quality control, and healthcare.

The Significance of Anomaly Detection

Anomalies can be indicators of critical events or issues that demand attention. They can signal fraudulent transactions, network intrusions, manufacturing defects, or even health anomalies in patients. Detecting these anomalies promptly is essential to prevent potential risks and mitigate damage. Anomaly detection helps organizations and systems maintain integrity, security, and quality.

Common Approaches to Anomaly Detection

1. **Statistical Methods**: Statistical techniques, such as Z-score, are used to identify anomalies based on the statistical properties of the data. Data points that deviate significantly from the mean or median are flagged as anomalies.
2. **Machine Learning**: Supervised and unsupervised machine learning techniques can be employed for anomaly detection. In supervised learning, anomalies are treated as a separate class, and models are trained to classify them. In unsupervised learning, anomalies are identified based on their deviation from the norm.
3. **Clustering**: Clustering algorithms like K-Means can be used to group similar data points together. Data points that do not fit well into any cluster may be considered anomalies.

4. **Density-Based Methods**: Density-based approaches, such as DBSCAN (Density-Based Spatial Clustering of Applications with Noise), identify anomalies as data points in low-density regions.
5. **Time-Series Analysis**: For time-dependent data, time-series analysis methods can be used to detect anomalies by modeling expected patterns and flagging deviations.

Challenges in Anomaly Detection

Anomaly detection comes with its own set of challenges:

- **Imbalanced Data**: In many real-world scenarios, anomalies are rare compared to normal data points, leading to class imbalance.
- **Feature Engineering**: Identifying relevant features and designing effective feature representations is crucial for accurate anomaly detection.
- **Model Selection**: Choosing the right algorithm and tuning its parameters can significantly impact the detection performance.
- **Dynamic Environments**: In dynamic systems, the concept of what is anomalous may change over time, requiring adaptive approaches.

Applications of Anomaly Detection

Anomaly detection has wide-ranging applications:

1. **Fraud Detection**: Identifying fraudulent transactions in finance and e-commerce, including credit card fraud and identity theft.
2. **Network Security**: Detecting unusual network traffic patterns indicative of cyberattacks or intrusions.
3. **Manufacturing Quality Control**: Identifying defects in products or processes on production lines.
4. **Healthcare**: Detecting anomalies in patient data to identify diseases or monitor the health status of individuals.

5. **Environmental Monitoring**: Identifying unusual readings in environmental sensors, such as pollution levels or temperature.
6. **Predictive Maintenance**: Detecting anomalies in machinery or equipment data to schedule maintenance before failures occur.

Recommender Systems

In an era of information overload and countless choices, recommender systems have emerged as a valuable tool for helping individuals discover relevant content, products, and services. These systems, often referred to as recommendation engines, leverage data and algorithms to provide personalized suggestions to users. Recommender systems have become ubiquitous, powering the recommendation features in platforms ranging from e-commerce websites to streaming services and content platforms.

The Role of Recommender Systems

Recommender systems address the challenge of information overload by assisting users in finding items of interest from a vast pool of options. Whether you're searching for a movie to watch, a book to read, or products to buy, recommender systems can significantly enhance your decision-making process.

Types of Recommender Systems

There are several approaches to building recommender systems, each with its own strengths and techniques. The primary types of recommender systems are:

1. **Collaborative Filtering**: Collaborative filtering relies on the behavior and preferences of users to make recommendations. It assumes that users who have interacted similarly with items in the past will continue to do so. Collaborative filtering can be further divided into user-based and item-based methods.

2. **Content-Based Filtering**: Content-based filtering recommends items to users based on the characteristics or content of items and the user's profile. For instance, if a user enjoys science fiction movies, a content-based recommender system will suggest other science fiction movies.

3. **Hybrid Recommender Systems**: Hybrid systems combine multiple recommendation techniques to provide more accurate and diverse recommendations. These systems leverage both collaborative and content-based filtering, as well as other approaches like matrix factorization.

4. **Matrix Factorization**: Matrix factorization methods aim to factorize the user-item interaction matrix into two lower-dimensional matrices representing latent factors for users and items. This approach is particularly effective for handling sparse data.

Challenges in Recommender Systems

Building effective recommender systems comes with several challenges:

- **Data Sparsity**: In many cases, the user-item interaction data is sparse, making it challenging to find meaningful patterns.
- **Cold Start Problem**: Recommender systems often struggle to make recommendations for new users or items with limited interaction history.
- **Scalability**: Handling large datasets and real-time recommendations can be computationally intensive.
- **Privacy Concerns**: Recommender systems must balance personalization with user privacy and data security.

Applications of Recommender Systems

Recommender systems find applications in various domains:

1. **E-commerce**: Recommending products based on user preferences and purchase history.
2. **Media Streaming**: Suggesting movies, TV shows, or music based on user viewing or listening habits.

3. **Social Media**: Recommending people to connect with or content to engage with on social networks.
4. **News and Content Platforms**: Suggesting articles, news, or blog posts based on user interests.
5. **Travel and Tourism**: Recommending hotels, destinations, or activities based on user preferences and past travel history.
6. **E-learning**: Recommending courses, educational resources, and study materials based on a learner's progress and interests.

DEEP LEARNING

Introduction to Neural Networks

In the quest to mimic the remarkable processing power of the human brain, neural networks have emerged as a foundational concept in artificial intelligence and machine learning. Neural networks, often referred to as artificial neural networks (ANNs), are a class of computational models inspired by the structure and function of the human brain's neural networks. These networks have the ability to learn complex patterns and relationships from data, making them a cornerstone of modern machine learning.

The Essence of Neural Networks

At its core, a neural network is a mathematical model composed of interconnected nodes, or artificial neurons. These neurons, organized in layers, are designed to process and transform information. Neural networks are particularly adept at solving problems that involve pattern recognition, classification, regression, and decision-making.

Key Components of a Neural Network:

1. **Input Layer**: This layer receives data or features as input and passes them to the subsequent layers.

2. **Hidden Layers**: These layers, often consisting of multiple neurons, process and transform the input data through complex mathematical operations. Deep neural networks have multiple hidden layers, giving rise to the term "deep learning."

3. **Weights and Activation Functions**: Each connection between neurons has an associated weight that determines its strength. Activation functions introduce non-linearity into the network, allowing it to model complex relationships.

4. **Output Layer**: The final layer produces the network's output, which can be a classification, regression, or other relevant result.

Learning in Neural Networks

The process of training a neural network involves adjusting the weights of connections to minimize the difference between the network's predictions and the actual outcomes (targets) in a training dataset. This is typically done using optimization algorithms, such as gradient descent. During training, the network learns to recognize patterns and relationships in the data, allowing it to generalize and make predictions on unseen data.

Types of Neural Networks:

1. **Feedforward Neural Networks (FNNs)**: The simplest form of neural networks, where information flows in one direction, from the input layer to the output layer. They are used for tasks like image classification and regression.

2. **Convolutional Neural Networks (CNNs)**: Specialized for image and spatial data, CNNs use convolutional layers to capture local patterns and hierarchies of features.

3. **Recurrent Neural Networks (RNNs)**: Suitable for sequential data, RNNs have connections that loop back on themselves, allowing them to model temporal dependencies. They are used in tasks like natural language processing and time series prediction.

4. **Long Short-Term Memory (LSTM) Networks**: A type of RNN designed to handle long-range dependencies and mitigate the vanishing gradient problem.
5. **Generative Adversarial Networks (GANs)**: Comprising a generator and a discriminator, GANs are used to generate new data samples, such as images, music, or text, that are indistinguishable from real data.

Applications of Neural Networks:

Neural networks find applications in a wide range of fields:

- **Computer Vision**: Recognizing objects, detecting anomalies, and image synthesis.
- **Natural Language Processing**: Language translation, chatbots, sentiment analysis, and speech recognition.
- **Autonomous Systems**: Self-driving cars, robotics, and drones use neural networks for perception and decision-making.
- **Healthcare**: Medical image analysis, disease diagnosis, and drug discovery.
- **Finance**: Predicting stock prices, fraud detection, and algorithmic trading.
- **Recommendation Systems**: Personalizing product recommendations on e-commerce platforms and content recommendations on streaming services.

Challenges and Opportunities

While neural networks have achieved remarkable success, they come with challenges such as the need for large datasets, substantial computational resources, and interpretability issues. Nevertheless, the opportunities they offer in terms of automation, pattern recognition, and problem-solving are vast, shaping the landscape of artificial intelligence and machine learning.

Building and Training Neural Networks

Neural networks, the fundamental building blocks of deep learning, are versatile and powerful tools for solving a wide range of complex problems. Building and training neural networks involves creating a model architecture, preparing data, and optimizing model parameters to make accurate predictions.

1. Model Architecture

The first step in building a neural network is defining its architecture. This includes specifying the number of layers, the type of layers, the number of neurons or units in each layer, and the activation functions. The choice of architecture depends on the specific problem you're trying to solve. Common architectures include:

- **Feedforward Neural Networks (FNNs)**: These consist of an input layer, one or more hidden layers, and an output layer. The neurons in each layer are fully connected to the neurons in the adjacent layers.
- **Convolutional Neural Networks (CNNs)**: Used for tasks involving images and spatial data, CNNs include convolutional layers for feature extraction and pooling layers for down-sampling.
- **Recurrent Neural Networks (RNNs)**: Suitable for sequential data, RNNs have connections that loop back on themselves, allowing them to model temporal dependencies.
- **Long Short-Term Memory (LSTM) Networks**: A specialized type of RNN designed to handle long-range dependencies and mitigate the vanishing gradient problem.

2. Data Preparation

Data preparation is a critical step in building and training neural networks. It involves:

- **Data Collection**: Gathering and curating a dataset that is representative of the problem you're addressing.

- **Data Preprocessing**: Cleaning and formatting the data, handling missing values, and scaling features to a common range.
- **Data Splitting**: Dividing the dataset into training, validation, and test sets to evaluate the model's performance.
- **Data Augmentation**: For image data, augmenting the dataset by applying transformations like rotation, cropping, and flipping to increase diversity.

3. Model Compilation

Once the architecture is defined, you need to compile the neural network. Compiling involves specifying the loss function, optimizer, and evaluation metrics:

- **Loss Function**: The loss function measures the difference between the predicted output and the true target values. Common loss functions include mean squared error for regression and categorical cross-entropy for classification.
- **Optimizer**: The optimizer adjusts the model's weights during training to minimize the loss. Popular optimizers include stochastic gradient descent (SGD), Adam, and RMSprop.
- **Metrics**: Evaluation metrics, such as accuracy, precision, recall, or F1-score, are chosen based on the problem type.

4. Training

Training a neural network involves feeding it with the training data, adjusting the model's weights through backpropagation, and iteratively updating the model to minimize the loss function. The training process consists of the following steps:

- **Forward Pass**: The input data is fed through the network, and predictions are made.
- **Loss Computation**: The loss is calculated by comparing the model's predictions to the actual target values.
- **Backpropagation**: Gradients are computed for each layer of the network using the chain rule of calculus, and the model's weights are updated accordingly.

- **Epochs and Batch Size**: Training is organized into epochs, with each epoch representing one complete pass through the training data. Data is typically divided into batches for more efficient training.
- **Validation**: After each epoch, the model's performance is evaluated on the validation data to monitor progress and prevent overfitting.
- **Early Stopping**: Training can be stopped early if the validation performance starts to degrade, preventing overfitting.

5. Hyperparameter Tuning

Fine-tuning the model's hyperparameters is an essential step in building an effective neural network. Hyperparameters include the learning rate, batch size, number of layers, number of neurons per layer, and more. Grid search or randomized search can be used to find the optimal set of hyperparameters.

6. Model Evaluation and Testing

After training, the model's performance is evaluated on a separate test dataset to assess its generalization ability. The choice of evaluation metrics depends on the problem type (e.g., accuracy for classification, mean squared error for regression).

7. Deployment

Once the neural network is trained and evaluated, it can be deployed in real-world applications. Deployment may involve integrating the model into a web service, mobile app, or other software systems.

Building and training neural networks can be an iterative process, involving experimentation with different architectures, hyperparameters, and data preprocessing techniques to achieve the desired performance. Neural networks are incredibly powerful tools, but their effectiveness relies on careful design, data preparation, and fine-tuning. With the right approach, neural networks can solve complex problems across various domains.

Convolutional Neural Networks (CNNs)

Convolutional Neural Networks, or CNNs, are a class of deep learning models designed specifically for tasks involving images and spatial data. CNNs have revolutionized computer vision, enabling machines to understand and interpret visual information, making them indispensable in a wide range of applications, from image classification and object detection to facial recognition and medical image analysis.

The Need for CNNs

In traditional neural networks (like feedforward neural networks), each neuron in one layer is connected to every neuron in the next layer. While this design works well for structured data, it becomes highly inefficient for tasks like image recognition, where local patterns and spatial relationships are crucial. This is where CNNs excel.

Key Components of CNNs

CNNs are characterized by several key components that enable them to effectively process and extract features from images:

1. **Convolutional Layers**: These layers apply convolution operations to the input data using a set of learnable filters or kernels. These filters slide over the input image to detect local patterns such as edges, textures, and shapes.
2. **Activation Functions**: Non-linear activation functions, like ReLU (Rectified Linear Unit), are applied after convolution to introduce non-linearity into the model.
3. **Pooling Layers**: Pooling layers (e.g., max-pooling) reduce the spatial dimensions of the data while retaining the most important information. This reduces computational complexity and helps invariance to small translations.
4. **Fully Connected Layers**: After extracting hierarchical features through convolution and pooling, CNNs often

conclude with one or more fully connected layers for making final predictions.

5. **Multiple Channels**: CNNs can process multi-channel input data, such as RGB images, where each channel represents a color (red, green, blue). Each channel is processed independently through separate convolutional filters.

Convolution Operation

The convolution operation involves sliding a filter over the input data, element-wise multiplying the filter values with the corresponding input values, and summing the results. This process helps identify patterns and features, such as edges or corners, in different parts of the input.

Pooling Operation

Pooling reduces the spatial dimensions of the data by selecting the maximum (max-pooling) or average (average-pooling) value within a local region. This operation reduces the computational load and creates a form of translation invariance, making the network less sensitive to small shifts in the input.

Hierarchical Feature Extraction

CNNs are designed to automatically learn hierarchical features from data. Lower layers capture basic features like edges and corners, while higher layers combine these basic features to represent more complex patterns, ultimately enabling the network to recognize objects and structures in images.

Applications of CNNs

CNNs find applications in various domains:

1. **Image Classification**: Identifying objects, animals, or scenes within images.
2. **Object Detection**: Locating and classifying multiple objects within an image, often with bounding boxes.

3. **Facial Recognition**: Recognizing and verifying individuals based on facial features.
4. **Medical Imaging**: Analyzing medical images for disease diagnosis, tumor detection, and more.
5. **Autonomous Vehicles**: Enabling self-driving cars to perceive their environment.
6. **Natural Language Processing**: Combining visual and textual information for tasks like image captioning.
7. **Artificial Intelligence Art**: Generating art, deepfakes, and creative content.

Challenges and Advances

Despite their effectiveness, CNNs have challenges, such as the need for large amounts of labeled data and extensive computational resources. Recent advances, including transfer learning and architectures like ResNet and Inception, have improved the efficiency and performance of CNNs, allowing them to tackle even more complex tasks with fewer resources.

Recurrent Neural Networks (RNNs)

Recurrent Neural Networks (RNNs) are a class of deep learning models designed for handling sequential data, where the order of data points matters. Unlike traditional feedforward neural networks, RNNs have connections that loop back on themselves, allowing them to maintain and utilize information from previous time steps. RNNs are widely used in natural language processing, time series analysis, speech recognition, and various other tasks that involve sequential data.

The Need for RNNs

While feedforward neural networks excel at tasks with fixed-size inputs and outputs, they fall short when dealing with sequences of varying lengths. RNNs, on the other hand, are designed to handle sequences of data by maintaining a hidden state that captures information from previous time steps. This makes RNNs well-suited for tasks like language modeling, sentiment analysis, and speech synthesis, where understanding context is essential.

Key Components of RNNs

RNNs consist of several key components:

1. **Hidden State**: The hidden state, also known as the memory, is a vector that holds information from previous time steps. It acts as the RNN's memory and influences the current output.
2. **Input at Each Time Step**: At each time step, the RNN takes an input (e.g., a word in a sentence or a data point in a time series) and combines it with the previous hidden state to update the current hidden state.
3. **Activation Function**: Non-linear activation functions, such as the hyperbolic tangent (tanh) or Rectified Linear Unit (ReLU), introduce non-linearity into the model.
4. **Output**: The RNN can produce an output at each time step, and the output can be used for prediction or fed back into the network.

Vanishing Gradient Problem

One challenge with traditional RNNs is the vanishing gradient problem. During training, gradients can become very small as they are backpropagated through time steps, causing the network to have difficulty learning long-range dependencies. To address this issue, more advanced RNN architectures, such as Long Short-Term Memory (LSTM) networks and Gated Recurrent Unit (GRU) networks, have been developed.

LSTM and GRU Networks

LSTM and GRU networks are specialized RNN variants that are better at capturing long-term dependencies. They incorporate gating mechanisms that control the flow of information in and out of the hidden state, making them capable of remembering important information over longer sequences. LSTMs have separate memory cells, input gates, forget gates, and output gates, while GRUs have simplified gating mechanisms.

Applications of RNNs

RNNs find applications in various domains:

1. **Natural Language Processing**: Language modeling, text generation, machine translation, and sentiment analysis.
2. **Time Series Analysis**: Financial forecasting, weather prediction, and stock market analysis.
3. **Speech Recognition**: Converting spoken language into text.
4. **Handwriting Recognition**: Recognizing and converting handwritten text into digital text.
5. **Music Generation**: Composing music and generating new tunes.
6. **Autonomous Systems**: Assisting in decision-making for self-driving cars and robots.

Challenges and Advances

While RNNs are powerful for sequential data, they have challenges, such as difficulties in parallelization and long training times. Recent advances in deep learning have introduced more efficient architectures and training techniques, allowing RNNs to be used in even more sophisticated applications.

Transfer Learning

Transfer learning is a machine learning technique that leverages knowledge gained from one task to improve performance on a different but related task. It is based on the idea that models pretrained on large datasets and complex tasks can be fine-tuned or adapted for specific tasks, saving time and resources while achieving better results. Transfer learning has become a cornerstone of deep learning and has significantly advanced the field of artificial intelligence.

Motivation for Transfer Learning

The motivation behind transfer learning is twofold:

1. **Data Efficiency**: Collecting and annotating large datasets can be expensive and time-consuming. Transfer learning allows models to generalize from one dataset to another, reducing the amount of labeled data required for training.
2. **Knowledge Transfer**: Complex tasks often share common features or representations with simpler tasks. Transfer learning enables the transfer of knowledge and features learned from one task to another, promoting faster convergence and improved performance.

Types of Transfer Learning

There are several types of transfer learning:

1. **Feature Extraction**: In feature extraction, a pretrained model is used as a fixed feature extractor. The early layers of the model (the convolutional layers in the case of deep neural networks) are used to extract relevant features from the input data. These features are then fed into a new model that is trained for the specific task.
2. **Fine-Tuning**: Fine-tuning involves taking a pretrained model and adjusting the weights of some or all layers to adapt it to the target task. This approach allows the model to learn task-specific patterns while retaining knowledge from the original training.
3. **Domain Adaptation**: Domain adaptation aims to transfer knowledge from a source domain to a target domain, even when the two domains have different distributions. It's commonly used when there is a domain shift between the training data and the target data.

Examples of Transfer Learning

Transfer learning is widely used in various domains:

1. **Image Classification**: Pretrained convolutional neural networks, such as VGG, ResNet, and Inception, have been fine-tuned for specific image classification tasks.
2. **Natural Language Processing (NLP)**: Models like BERT and GPT have pretrained language representations that can be fine-tuned for tasks like sentiment analysis, named entity recognition, and machine translation.
3. **Computer Vision**: Transfer learning is used in object detection, image segmentation, and facial recognition.
4. **Healthcare**: Models pretrained on medical imaging data can be fine-tuned for specific diagnosis tasks.
5. **Recommendation Systems**: Collaborative filtering models can be improved by incorporating information from user behavior on related items.

Challenges in Transfer Learning

While transfer learning is a powerful tool, it comes with challenges:

1. **Domain Gap**: The source and target domains may have significant differences, leading to a domain gap. Adaptation techniques are used to bridge this gap.
2. **Overfitting**: Fine-tuning a model with a small target dataset can lead to overfitting. Regularization techniques and data augmentation are used to mitigate this issue.
3. **Task Selection**: Choosing an appropriate source task and model architecture is crucial for effective transfer learning.

MODEL DEPLOYMENT AND PRACTICAL CONSIDERATIONS

Model Deployment and Serving

Model deployment and serving are critical steps in the machine learning lifecycle, where the well-crafted models transition from the development environment to real-world applications. In this phase, models are made available to users or systems, allowing them to make predictions and generate insights. Successful deployment and serving ensure that the models perform reliably, efficiently, and securely in production environments.

The Importance of Deployment and Serving

Model deployment is the bridge between model development and its practical use. It's where the rubber meets the road, and models start adding value. Here are some key aspects of why model deployment and serving are crucial:

1. **Real-World Impact**: Deployed models have the potential to affect real-world decisions and actions, from recommending products to medical diagnoses, autonomous driving, and more.

2. **User Accessibility**: Deployed models are accessible to end-users, whether they are customers, healthcare professionals, or engineers, enabling them to leverage the model's predictions or recommendations.
3. **Continual Learning**: Real-world deployment provides an opportunity for models to learn and adapt to changing data distributions, ensuring that they remain effective over time.

Challenges and Considerations

Model deployment and serving come with various challenges and considerations:

1. **Scalability**: Ensuring that the deployed model can handle a large number of requests efficiently, often requiring strategies like load balancing and distributed computing.
2. **Latency**: Minimizing inference latency is crucial, especially in applications where real-time responses are required, such as autonomous vehicles and financial trading systems.
3. **Security**: Protecting models from adversarial attacks and ensuring the security of sensitive data are paramount.
4. **Versioning**: Managing model versions and rolling out updates smoothly without disrupting services.
5. **Monitoring**: Implementing monitoring and logging to detect model drift, anomalies, and performance issues.
6. **Resource Management**: Efficiently managing hardware resources, such as GPUs, to optimize model serving.

Deployment Environments

The choice of deployment environment depends on the specific application requirements:

1. **Cloud Services**: Cloud platforms like AWS, Azure, and Google Cloud provide scalable, managed environments for deploying machine learning models. They offer a range of services, including AWS SageMaker, Azure Machine Learning, and Google Cloud AI Platform.

2. **Edge Devices**: In edge computing, models are deployed directly on devices like smartphones, IoT devices, and edge servers. Edge deployment reduces latency and enables offline functionality but requires efficient model architectures due to resource constraints.

3. **Embedded Systems**: In scenarios where models need to run on resource-constrained embedded devices, model quantization and optimization become essential.

4. **Containers and Orchestration**: Technologies like Docker and Kubernetes simplify the deployment and scaling of models within containers, making it easier to manage multiple deployments.

Model Serving

Model serving is the process of exposing machine learning models as APIs or services that can be queried to obtain predictions. Key considerations in model serving include:

1. **API Design**: Creating a user-friendly API that allows clients to send input data and receive model predictions in a standardized format.

2. **Load Balancing**: Distributing incoming requests among multiple instances of the model to ensure scalability and fault tolerance.

3. **Caching**: Implementing caching mechanisms to store frequently used data or predictions, reducing computational load.

4. **Authentication and Authorization**: Ensuring that only authorized users or systems can access the model API to protect sensitive information.

Versioning and Continuous Deployment

Managing different versions of models is essential to facilitate model updates and maintain a consistent user experience. Techniques such as blue-green deployment and canary releases allow for controlled and gradual model updates.

Monitoring and Maintenance

Once a machine learning model is deployed in a real-world environment, the journey is far from over. Monitoring and maintenance are critical aspects of ensuring that the model continues to perform accurately, efficiently, and securely. This ongoing process is essential for preventing issues, adapting to changing conditions, and maximizing the model's utility.

Why Monitoring and Maintenance Matter

Monitoring and maintenance are essential for several reasons:

1. **Model Drift**: The real-world data distribution can change over time, leading to a phenomenon known as "model drift." This means that the model's predictions may become less accurate as it encounters new data patterns. Monitoring helps detect and address drift.
2. **Performance Degradation**: Over time, models can experience performance degradation due to various factors, including changes in data quality or hardware issues. Monitoring ensures that models continue to meet performance expectations.
3. **Security**: Monitoring helps identify potential security vulnerabilities and risks, such as adversarial attacks or unauthorized access to the model.
4. **Resource Management**: Monitoring resource usage, such as CPU, memory, and GPU, is crucial for optimizing costs and preventing resource exhaustion.

Key Aspects of Monitoring and Maintenance

Effective monitoring and maintenance involve several key aspects:

1. **Data Quality**: Regularly assess the quality of input data. Data anomalies or inconsistencies can adversely affect model performance. Implement data validation and cleaning processes to ensure data integrity.

2. **Model Performance Metrics**: Define relevant performance metrics and continuously monitor them. Metrics may include accuracy, precision, recall, F1-score, and any domain-specific metrics related to your application.
3. **Data Drift Detection**: Use statistical methods and drift detection techniques to identify changes in the data distribution. When drift is detected, retraining the model with updated data may be necessary.
4. **Performance Thresholds**: Establish performance thresholds or alerts. When metrics fall below acceptable levels, automated notifications can trigger model retraining or other corrective actions.
5. **Security Auditing**: Regularly audit security measures to protect the model from potential attacks. Implement authentication, authorization, and encryption mechanisms to safeguard sensitive data.
6. **Resource Monitoring**: Continuously monitor resource usage to prevent resource bottlenecks and overutilization. Scaling resources up or down as needed can help maintain efficient model serving.
7. **Logging and Error Handling**: Maintain comprehensive logs of model interactions, including input data, predictions, and errors. Logs are invaluable for troubleshooting and auditing.
8. **Version Control**: Keep track of model versions and maintain a version history. This allows for seamless rollback in case of issues with newer versions.

Automated Monitoring and Alerting

To streamline monitoring and maintenance, consider implementing automated systems that can:

1. **Generate Alerts**: Automated alerting systems can notify relevant personnel or teams when predefined thresholds are breached.
2. **Scheduled Checks**: Set up scheduled checks and automated tests to evaluate model performance and data quality at regular intervals.

3. **Model Retraining**: Automate the process of retraining models when drift or performance degradation is detected.
4. **Resource Scaling**: Use auto-scaling mechanisms to dynamically allocate resources based on usage patterns.

Continuous Improvement

Monitoring and maintenance should not be seen as a one-time task but as an ongoing process of continuous improvement. Regularly review the monitoring data, adjust thresholds, and update the model as needed. Keep in mind that the deployment environment, data, and user requirements can evolve, necessitating adaptation and refinement.

Ethical and Responsible AI

As artificial intelligence (AI) continues to advance and permeate various aspects of our lives, it brings with it a range of ethical and societal considerations. Ensuring that AI is developed and deployed responsibly is crucial to avoid harm, protect individuals' rights, and build trust in AI systems. Ethical and responsible AI encompasses a set of principles, guidelines, and practices aimed at addressing these concerns.

Why Ethical and Responsible AI Matters

1. **Bias and Fairness**: AI systems can inherit biases present in training data, leading to unfair outcomes, discrimination, and reinforcing societal inequalities.
2. **Privacy**: AI often involves the collection and analysis of vast amounts of personal data, raising privacy concerns if not handled responsibly.
3. **Transparency**: Lack of transparency in AI decision-making processes can undermine trust and accountability, making it essential to understand how AI systems arrive at their conclusions.

4. **Accountability**: Determining who is responsible when AI systems make decisions or cause harm is a complex challenge that ethical guidelines seek to address.

Key Principles of Ethical and Responsible AI

1. **Fairness**: AI systems should be designed and trained to ensure fairness and avoid bias, particularly in decision-making processes that impact individuals or groups.
2. **Transparency**: Developers and organizations should strive for transparency in AI systems, providing clear explanations of how decisions are made and the factors influencing those decisions.
3. **Accountability**: Clear lines of responsibility should be established for AI systems, and mechanisms for holding individuals or organizations accountable for AI-related actions should be in place.
4. **Privacy**: Privacy should be respected throughout the AI lifecycle, from data collection to storage and usage, with data anonymization and encryption practices in place.
5. **Security**: AI systems should be designed with security in mind to prevent vulnerabilities and protect against malicious use.

Real-World Applications of Ethical and Responsible AI

1. **Algorithmic Bias Mitigation**: Techniques such as re-sampling, re-weighting, and fairness-aware training are used to reduce bias and ensure fairness in AI models, particularly in areas like hiring and lending.
2. **Data Privacy**: Organizations implement data anonymization, data minimization, and consent mechanisms to protect user privacy in AI applications, particularly in healthcare and finance.
3. **Explainable AI (XAI)**: Researchers work on developing AI systems that provide understandable explanations for their decisions, enhancing transparency and trust.

4. **AI Ethics Committees**: Some organizations establish committees or boards to review and assess the ethical implications of AI projects and make recommendations.

Challenges and Considerations

1. **Data Quality**: Ensuring high-quality, unbiased training data is challenging, especially when historical data contains biases.
2. **Regulations and Standards**: Ethical and responsible AI practices often intersect with regulations like the General Data Protection Regulation (GDPR) and the development of industry standards.
3. **Global Perspective**: Ethical AI must consider cultural and societal differences, as what is considered ethical can vary across regions and communities.

The Role of AI Developers and Organizations

Developers and organizations involved in AI should:

1. **Educate and Train**: Invest in education and training programs to ensure AI professionals understand the ethical implications and responsibilities associated with AI development.
2. **Ethics by Design**: Incorporate ethical considerations from the outset of AI projects and continually assess and mitigate ethical risks.
3. **Collaborate**: Work with multidisciplinary teams that include ethicists, lawyers, and domain experts to make informed ethical decisions.
4. **Engage with Stakeholders**: Seek input and feedback from stakeholders, including those who may be affected by AI decisions.
5. **Regular Audits**: Conduct regular audits and assessments of AI systems to ensure ongoing compliance with ethical and responsible AI principles.

FUTURE TRENDS AND ADVANCED TOPICS

Reinforcement Learning

Reinforcement Learning (RL) is a subfield of machine learning that focuses on training algorithms to make sequences of decisions. Unlike supervised learning, where models learn from labeled data, or unsupervised learning, where models find patterns in unlabeled data, RL agents learn through trial and error in an environment. It is a powerful approach for solving problems that involve sequential decision-making, such as robotics, game playing, autonomous systems, and recommendation systems.

Key Concepts in Reinforcement Learning

1. **Agent**: The learner or decision-maker that interacts with the environment.
2. **Environment**: The external system or world with which the agent interacts. It includes everything that the agent doesn't control.
3. **State (s)**: A representation of the environment at a particular time. It encapsulates all relevant information needed to make decisions.

4. **Action (a)**: The choices or decisions made by the agent that affect the environment.
5. **Policy (π)**: The strategy or mapping from states to actions, which defines the agent's behavior. It represents the agent's way of making decisions.
6. **Reward (r)**: A numerical value provided by the environment to evaluate the agent's actions. The reward signals whether an action is good or bad.
7. **Value Function (V)**: The expected cumulative reward an agent can achieve starting from a particular state and following a policy. It helps the agent evaluate how good it is to be in a particular state.
8. **Q-Value Function (Q)**: Similar to the value function but takes into account both the state and the action. It estimates the expected cumulative reward of taking a specific action in a given state.

The RL Learning Process

The RL learning process is often described as a cycle:

1. **Initialization**: The agent and environment are set up, and initial states and policies are defined.
2. **Interaction**: The agent takes actions in the environment, leading to state transitions and receiving rewards.
3. **Learning**: The agent updates its policy based on the received rewards and the evaluation of the state-action pairs.
4. **Execution**: The updated policy is used to make decisions in the environment.
5. **Repeat**: The cycle continues iteratively, allowing the agent to improve its policy over time.

Exploration vs. Exploitation

One of the core challenges in RL is the exploration-exploitation trade-off. Agents need to explore new actions to learn about their consequences (exploration) while also exploiting their current knowledge to maximize rewards (exploitation). Balancing these two aspects is crucial for effective learning.

Reinforcement Learning Algorithms

Several RL algorithms are used to train agents, including:

1. **Q-Learning**: An off-policy RL algorithm that learns the Q-value function to estimate action values.
2. **Deep Q-Networks (DQN)**: Combines Q-learning with deep neural networks to handle high-dimensional state spaces.
3. **Policy Gradients**: Directly optimize policies by maximizing expected rewards. Methods like REINFORCE and Proximal Policy Optimization (PPO) fall under this category.
4. **Actor-Critic**: Combines value estimation (critic) with policy improvement (actor) to stabilize and accelerate learning.
5. **Model-Based RL**: Builds a model of the environment and uses it for planning and decision-making.

Applications of Reinforcement Learning

Reinforcement learning has found applications in various domains:

1. **Game Playing**: RL has been used to create AI agents that excel in complex games like chess, Go, and video games.
2. **Robotics**: RL is used to train robots to perform tasks such as navigation, manipulation, and even walking.
3. **Recommendation Systems**: RL can personalize recommendations for users in online platforms.
4. **Autonomous Vehicles**: RL is applied in self-driving cars and drones for decision-making and control.
5. **Healthcare**: RL aids in optimizing treatment plans and drug discovery.
6. **Finance**: RL is used for portfolio management, algorithmic trading, and risk assessment.
7. **Natural Language Processing**: Conversational AI and dialogue systems use RL for dialogue management.
8. **Energy Management**: RL optimizes energy consumption in smart grids and buildings.

Reinforcement learning continues to be an active area of research, with the potential to solve complex real-world problems. It offers exciting opportunities for advancing AI and autonomous systems, making them more capable of learning and adapting to dynamic environments.

Generative Adversarial Networks (GANs)

Generative Adversarial Networks (GANs) are a class of deep learning models introduced by Ian Goodfellow and his colleagues in 2014. GANs have gained immense popularity for their ability to generate realistic data, whether it be images, text, or other types of content. They consist of two neural networks, a generator and a discriminator, engaged in a dynamic adversarial training process.

Key Components of GANs

1. **Generator**: The generator network takes random noise or a seed as input and produces synthetic data as output. It learns to create data that is indistinguishable from real data. In image generation, for example, the generator learns to produce images that resemble the dataset it was trained on.
2. **Discriminator**: The discriminator network acts as a binary classifier. Its job is to distinguish between real data (from the training dataset) and fake data generated by the generator. It provides feedback to the generator to help it improve its output.
3. **Adversarial Process**: GANs operate through a two-player minimax game. The generator aims to produce data that is so realistic that the discriminator cannot differentiate between real and fake data. The discriminator's objective is to become better at distinguishing real from fake data.

Training Process

The training of GANs follows these steps:

1. **Initialization**: Both the generator and discriminator are initialized with random weights.
2. **Generator Output**: The generator produces fake data from random noise.
3. **Discriminator Input**: The discriminator is fed with a combination of real data from the training dataset and fake data from the generator.
4. **Discriminator Training**: The discriminator is trained to classify real and fake data correctly by updating its weights. It minimizes its loss when classifying real data as "real" and fake data as "fake."
5. **Generator Training**: The generator is trained to produce data that the discriminator classifies as real. It aims to maximize the loss of the discriminator. In other words, the generator tries to generate data that is indistinguishable from real data.
6. **Iterative Process**: Steps 3-5 are repeated iteratively. The generator gets better at creating realistic data, and the discriminator becomes more accurate at distinguishing real from fake data.

Applications of GANs

GANs have found a wide range of applications in various domains:

1. **Image Generation**: GANs have been used to create realistic images, art, and graphics. They have applications in generating high-resolution images, creating deepfakes, and even generating images from textual descriptions.
2. **Data Augmentation**: GANs can generate additional data samples to augment training datasets, especially in situations where collecting more real data is challenging or expensive.
3. **Style Transfer**: GANs are used in style transfer applications to transform images in the style of famous artists or to apply artistic styles to photographs.
4. **Super-Resolution**: GANs can enhance the resolution and quality of images and videos, which is beneficial in applications like medical imaging and video compression.

5. **Image-to-Image Translation**: GANs can perform tasks like turning sketches into realistic images, converting black and white photos to color, and translating satellite images to maps.
6. **Text-to-Image Synthesis**: GANs can generate images from textual descriptions, enabling creative storytelling and content generation.
7. **Drug Discovery**: GANs are used to generate molecular structures for drug discovery and materials science.
8. **Anomaly Detection**: GANs can learn normal data distributions and identify anomalies, which is valuable in fraud detection and quality control.

Challenges and Considerations

While GANs have shown remarkable capabilities, they also present challenges:

1. **Mode Collapse**: In some cases, the generator may produce a limited variety of outputs, known as mode collapse.
2. **Training Instability**: GAN training can be unstable, and finding the right balance between generator and discriminator training can be challenging.
3. **Evaluation**: Evaluating the quality and diversity of generated samples remains an active research area.
4. **Ethical Concerns**: GANs can be used for malicious purposes, such as generating deepfakes or counterfeit content, raising ethical concerns.

Generative Adversarial Networks continue to be an exciting area of research with the potential to revolutionize content generation and data augmentation across various domains. As techniques and architectures evolve, GANs are likely to play an increasingly prominent role in AI and creative applications.

Natural Language Processing (NLP)

Natural Language Processing (NLP) is a branch of artificial intelligence (AI) that focuses on the interaction between computers and human language. It seeks to enable machines to understand, interpret, and generate human language in a way that is both valuable and meaningful. NLP is a multidisciplinary field that combines elements of computer science, linguistics, and machine learning to bridge the gap between human communication and computing systems.

Key Components of Natural Language Processing

1. **Text Analysis**: At the core of NLP is the analysis of text data. This involves tasks such as tokenization (breaking text into words or phrases), part-of-speech tagging (identifying the grammatical category of each word), and parsing (analyzing the grammatical structure of sentences).
2. **Information Retrieval**: NLP is used to retrieve specific information from large textual datasets. Search engines like Google utilize NLP techniques to deliver relevant search results based on user queries.
3. **Machine Translation**: NLP is responsible for machine translation systems like Google Translate, which automatically translate text from one language to another.
4. **Sentiment Analysis**: Sentiment analysis, or opinion mining, assesses the sentiment or emotion expressed in text data. This is commonly used to gauge public opinion on social media, product reviews, and news articles.
5. **Named Entity Recognition (NER)**: NER is the process of identifying and classifying named entities in text, such as names of people, places, organizations, and dates.
6. **Speech Recognition**: NLP powers speech recognition systems that convert spoken language into text. Virtual assistants like Siri and Alexa rely on NLP to understand and respond to voice commands.

Challenges in Natural Language Processing

NLP presents several challenges due to the inherent complexity of human language:

1. **Ambiguity**: Natural language is often ambiguous, with words and phrases having multiple meanings based on context. NLP models must disambiguate and understand context.
2. **Variability**: Language is highly variable, with dialects, slang, and regional differences. NLP systems need to be robust to these variations.
3. **Context**: Understanding context is crucial for accurate language comprehension. This includes understanding the relationship between words in a sentence and the broader context of a conversation or document.
4. **Lack of Formal Rules**: Unlike programming languages, natural language lacks strict, formal rules, making it challenging to develop algorithms that consistently understand and generate text.

Applications of Natural Language Processing

NLP has a wide range of applications across various domains:

1. **Chatbots and Virtual Assistants**: NLP powers conversational agents that provide customer support, answer questions, and perform tasks via text or speech interactions.
2. **Language Translation**: NLP enables automatic translation between languages, facilitating global communication.
3. **Sentiment Analysis**: Businesses use sentiment analysis to understand customer opinions, assess brand perception, and make data-driven decisions.
4. **Content Summarization**: NLP is used to automatically generate concise summaries of lengthy documents, making information more accessible.
5. **Information Extraction**: NLP helps extract structured information from unstructured text, such as extracting named entities or key facts from news articles.
6. **Language Generation**: NLP models can generate human-like text, which is used in content generation, creative writing, and even code generation.

7. **Healthcare:** NLP assists in medical record analysis, clinical documentation, and medical research by extracting valuable insights from patient data.
8. **Legal and Compliance:** Legal professionals use NLP for contract analysis, legal document review, and compliance monitoring.

Recent Advances in NLP

Recent advancements in NLP have been driven by deep learning techniques, particularly transformer-based models like BERT (Bidirectional Encoder Representations from Transformers) and GPT (Generative Pre-trained Transformer). These models have achieved state-of-the-art results in various NLP tasks, making significant strides in language understanding and generation.

Quantum Machine Learning

Quantum Machine Learning (QML) is an emerging interdisciplinary field that combines quantum computing and machine learning techniques. It leverages the unique properties of quantum computers, such as superposition and entanglement, to perform machine learning tasks more efficiently and solve complex problems that are infeasible for classical computers. QML represents a promising frontier at the intersection of quantum physics and artificial intelligence.

Key Concepts in Quantum Machine Learning

1. **Quantum Bits (Qubits):** Unlike classical bits that can represent either 0 or 1, qubits can exist in a superposition of states, allowing quantum computers to process multiple possibilities simultaneously. This enables exponential speedup for certain algorithms.
2. **Quantum Entanglement:** Qubits can become entangled, meaning their states are interconnected. Changes to one qubit instantly affect the state of the other, even when separated by

vast distances. This property can be harnessed in quantum algorithms for optimization and search tasks.

3. **Quantum Gates**: Quantum gates are the quantum equivalent of classical logic gates, used to manipulate qubits. Operations like the Hadamard gate and CNOT gate are fundamental to quantum algorithms.

Quantum Algorithms for Machine Learning

Several quantum algorithms and techniques have been developed for machine learning tasks:

1. **Quantum Support Vector Machines (QSVM)**: QSVMs use quantum circuits to implement SVM classifiers, potentially providing a speedup in classifying data.
2. **Quantum Neural Networks**: Quantum neural networks use quantum gates to perform computations in neural networks, enabling quantum acceleration for deep learning tasks.
3. **Quantum Principal Component Analysis (PCA)**: Quantum PCA can find principal components of high-dimensional data more efficiently than classical PCA.
4. **Quantum Clustering**: Quantum algorithms can be applied to clustering tasks, providing potential speedup for grouping similar data points.
5. **Quantum Optimization**: Quantum algorithms, like the Quantum Approximate Optimization Algorithm (QAOA), can be used for combinatorial optimization problems common in machine learning.

Challenges and Considerations

Quantum Machine Learning is still in its infancy and faces several challenges:

1. **Quantum Hardware Limitations**: Building and maintaining quantum computers with a sufficient number of qubits and low error rates is a significant challenge.
2. **Quantum Error Correction**: Quantum systems are susceptible to errors due to decoherence and noise.

Developing effective error correction codes is crucial for the reliability of quantum algorithms.

3. **Hybrid Approaches**: Most quantum machine learning approaches are currently hybrid, where classical computers handle pre-processing and post-processing tasks due to the limitations of current quantum hardware.

Applications of Quantum Machine Learning

While quantum computers are not yet widely available for practical use, they hold the potential to transform various industries:

1. **Drug Discovery**: QML can simulate molecular interactions more accurately, accelerating drug discovery processes.
2. **Financial Modeling**: Quantum computing can optimize portfolios, perform risk analysis, and improve financial modeling.
3. **Cryptography**: Quantum computing poses a threat to classical cryptography. QML can be used to develop quantum-safe encryption methods.
4. **Supply Chain Optimization**: Quantum optimization algorithms can optimize complex supply chain logistics, minimizing costs and improving efficiency.
5. **Machine Learning Speedup**: Quantum acceleration can enhance machine learning models, making them more efficient for tasks like image recognition and natural language processing.
6. **Climate Modeling**: Quantum computing can help simulate complex climate models, contributing to climate change research.

The Future of Machine Learning

Machine learning has witnessed remarkable growth and transformation since its inception, and its future promises to be even more dynamic and influential. As technology advances and new research emerges, the future of machine learning holds several key trends and developments:

1. Explainable AI (XAI): As machine learning models become increasingly complex, there is a growing need for transparency and interpretability. XAI focuses on creating models that can provide understandable explanations for their decisions, which is crucial for applications like healthcare, finance, and legal systems.

2. Federated Learning: Privacy concerns are driving the development of federated learning, where machine learning models are trained collaboratively across multiple decentralized devices or servers without exchanging raw data. This approach ensures data privacy while still enabling model improvements.

3. AI Ethics and Responsible AI: Ethical considerations surrounding AI and machine learning are gaining prominence. The future will see more emphasis on ethical guidelines, regulations, and frameworks to ensure AI systems are developed and deployed responsibly.

4. Quantum Machine Learning: Quantum computing has the potential to revolutionize machine learning by providing exponential speedup for certain algorithms. As quantum hardware becomes more accessible, quantum machine learning will unlock new possibilities for solving complex problems.

5. Reinforcement Learning Advancements: Reinforcement learning is expected to advance significantly, enabling machines to master a wider range of tasks and exhibit human-level performance in areas such as robotics, autonomous systems, and game playing.

6. Transfer Learning and Few-Shot Learning: Improvements in transfer learning techniques will allow models to transfer knowledge from one domain to another, requiring less labeled data. Few-shot learning will enable models to learn from very few examples, making them more adaptable.

7. AI for Scientific Discovery: Machine learning will continue to play a crucial role in accelerating scientific discovery, from drug development and material science to climate modeling and particle physics.

8. Natural Language Processing Breakthroughs: Natural language understanding and generation will advance, enabling more sophisticated applications in chatbots, virtual assistants, language translation, and content generation.

9. Edge AI: The deployment of AI models directly on edge devices, such as IoT sensors and mobile devices, will become more prevalent, reducing latency and improving real-time decision-making in various applications.

10. Human-AI Collaboration: The future of machine learning is not about replacing humans but augmenting their capabilities. Human-AI collaboration will become more seamless and productive, enabling humans to leverage AI as a powerful tool in various domains.

11. AI in Healthcare: Machine learning will continue to transform healthcare by improving diagnosis, treatment planning, drug discovery, and patient care. Personalized medicine, driven by AI, will become more prevalent.

12. Autonomous Systems: Machine learning will enable the development of highly autonomous systems, from self-driving cars and drones to robotic assistants, with improved safety and reliability.

13. Ethical Considerations and Regulation: As AI and machine learning become more integrated into society, governments and organizations will implement stricter regulations and standards to address ethical concerns, data privacy, and algorithmic bias.

The future of machine learning is a convergence of cutting-edge technology, ethical considerations, and human ingenuity. It holds the potential to revolutionize industries, drive innovation, and address complex challenges. As researchers, engineers, and policymakers work together, the future of machine learning promises a more connected, efficient, and ethical world powered by intelligent machines.